Cornwall's
HISTORIC BUILDINGS

Cornwall's
Historic Buildings

Joan Rendell

First published 2008

The History Press
The Mill, Brimscombe Port
Stroud, Gloucestershire, GL5 2QG
www.thehistorypress.co.uk

British Library Cataloguing in Publication Data.
A catalogue record for this book is available from the British Library.

ISBN 978 0 7509 5041 1

Typesetting and origination by The History Press
Printed in Great Britain

Contents

fOREWORD

This is Joan's thirtieth book and, if it carries a fraction of the infectious enthusiasm and knowledge of her twenty-ninth, it will be another personal triumph for her. Once more the subject is her beloved Cornwall and anyone interested in the buildings of this historic county is sure to find much pleasure within its pages.

Fifty years ago Joan was made a Member of the Order of the British Empire, so it seems fitting that this work should mark the half-century of her being honoured with that prestigious award. On a more personal note, she has written for *Period House* over a number of years and her contributions have been a constant delight. I wish her every success with her latest book.

George Player
Editor, *Period House*

Introduction

Cornwall has been described by one well-known writer as being 'awash with historic buildings.' Perhaps that is a slight exaggeration, but certainly the county is rich in buildings which have survived the centuries, each with its own interesting history, from stately homes to humble cottages, from the reconstruction of a Bronze-Age dwelling to structures to assist seafarers around our notoriously dangerous coasts. As the reader goes through this book they will see how buildings have developed through the ages from the Bronze-Age North Hill to the ultra-modern 'underground' house in north Cornwall.

Unless otherwise credited in Acknowledgements, all photographs are from my own collection.

Joan Rendell
Launceston, Cornwall

acknowledgements

I am deeply indebted to the following for the use of photographs and/or information; John Neale; John Lyne; Gerald Fry; James Trewin, Trewin Design Partnership; Anne Philp; Bob Acton; The National Trust; Ruth Gilmore, Tamar Protection Society; Mrs S. Marriott, Cornwall Heritage Trust; the staff at Launceston County Branch Library; Guy Evans; Sarah Gruzdev; Partick Aubery-Fletcher; Mark at Cornwall County Reference & Information Library; Phil Glew Photography; Dr Bill Johnson; also the late Michael Trinick and the late Betty Worden. Without their valuable help this book could not have been produced.

An A-Z of
Cornwall's Historic Buildings

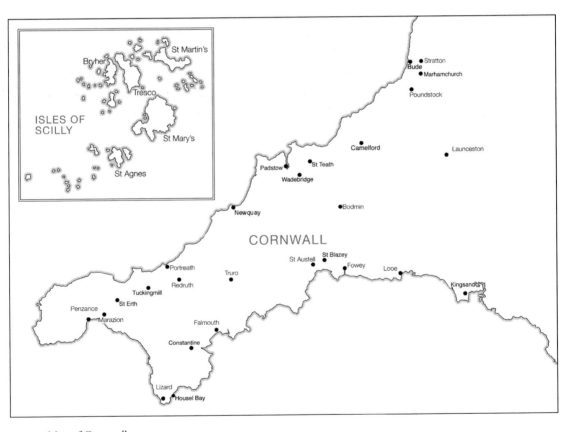

Map of Cornwall.

altarnun

Codda – a medieval homestead

There are quite a few ancient farmsteads on Bodmin Moor, but possibly none more steeped in history that Codda in the parish of Altarnun, in the heart of the moor. The moor is a delightful area on sunny summer days, but inhospitable and almost menacing in the winter when the snow is falling, and some dwellings can be completely cut off from main roads.

Codda is believed to have originated as a longhouse in medieval times, and the structure would have housed both humans and animals under the same roof, with a passage through the middle separating the two sets of inhabitants. It is thought that it was one of four homesteads in a medieval hamlet, the inhabitants of which worked the strop fields which, rather amazingly, still survive beyond the margins of the nineteenth-century field system – testimony to the remoteness of the setting.

The longhouses mangers were discovered in a thorough and painstaking survey by the then Cornwall Archaeological Unit (now the Historic Environment Department of Cornwall County Council). However, the original mangers were overlain by eighteenth-century walling and stabling, and footing of one metre wide walls were uncovered.

In the seventeenth century, Codda was a substantial farmhouse and many moulded granite stone survive in-situ. When the Rodd family of Trebartha, North Hill became the new landlords in the mid-nineteenth century, the house was extended and field boundaries rebuilt. However, over the years Codda declined in importance and by the 1970s was no longer used as a farmstead, the fields being worked from another remote farm.

The whole complex was obviously originally carefully positioned on south-facing slopes on the north side of a sheltered side valley of the River Fowey, near the centre of the remote and almost entirely cut-off Bodmin Moor. It was strategically positioned by a stream and then, as now, the only access was across stepping stones through a very damp, and indeed boggy, meadow.

The earliest surviving documentary reference to Codda dates to 1239, although it is believed it may have been one of the first re-colonising settlements of the turn of the first millennium AD. By the thirteenth and fourteenth centuries it was part of a typical small hamlet of co-operating households and, strangely, it still exudes the atmosphere of its much, much earlier life. In 1280 it was referred to as 'Stuncodda' in the Assize Roll and in 1362 as 'Stemcodda'.

The history of Codda and the land surrounding it goes back such a long way that it is far too complicated to list in detail here. It is, however, interesting to note that Codda probably had top rating in the late seventeenth century, when a rate 'for repairing and maintaining of the

church' of Altarnun included the almost unbeatable sum of 6*d* each from Jane Dennie, widow, and Nicholas Speare, both of Codda. Only five of the forty-two people who contributed gave more than that 'magnificent' sum given by the two Codda residents. The affluence was probably demonstrated by the quality of the seventeenth-century shaped granite still surviving today in the farmhouse.

The whole site still retains many of the features from medieval times onwards, which make it a unique Cornish group of buildings. Codda is privately owned and access is not easy; only a four-by-four vehicle can negotiate it satisfactorily.

Baldhu

Billy Bray's 'Three Eyes' Chapel

Billy Bray may only have been a humble Cornish copper miner, but he was a man of vision and great dedication. He is the stuff of legend in Cornwall, and so is his 'Three Eyes' Chapel, a small, low building with three windows in a row. According to Chris Wright, in his book *Billy Bray in His Own Words*, Billy built his chapel 'in the face of mockery and ill feeling', but Billy pressed ahead with his usual determination and his belief that he was guided by the Lord.

William Trewartha Bray was born in 1794 in Twelveheads in the parish of Kea, near Truro. Billy's grandfather was a devout Methodist but Billy admits in his own *Journal* to leading 'a bad life' in his young days. He explains that he lived in Cornwall until the age of seventeen, when he moved to Devon and fell into the company of drunkards and misfits until he underwent a dramatic conversion after reading John Bunyan's book *Visions of Heaven and Hell*.

What he read had such a profound effect on him that he joined the Bible Christian movement and became famous in Cornwall as a local preacher, visiting chapels to enthral congregations with his fiery sermons. He wanted everyone to hear and appreciate his message and in 1830 he undertook the massive task of building his first chapel. For a poor working man with little money it must have seemed an almost impossible task. However, supporters contributed to the cost and to the actual building work. Billy himself took part, digging out the foundations which were close to the house where he lived. He called his first building project Bethel Chapel. That original building no longer exists; a mound in a field is the only reminder of it.

Billy's motto was 'the Lord will provide' and his second chapel-building project was at Kerley Downs, a building which soon got the nickname 'Three Eyes' because of its three windows.

Not content with that, Billy went on to build a third chapel, at Carharrack, near Redruth, which he named Great Deliverance and which opened in about 1840. Little is left of that chapel but the covered shell in a field that is currently used as a cowshed.

The 'Three Eyes' Chapel at Kerley Downs is still in use, although not on a regular basis. It actually closed in 1982, but such an historic building could not be left to rot away; Methodists throughout Cornwall and elsewhere rallied around and it was rededicated in 1984 as a memorial to Billy Bray himself, and several special services are held there each year. It is also a place of pilgrimage for Methodists from across the globe. It is now supported by the Billy Bray Memorial Trust, consisting of a group of Methodist trustees.

Billy Bray died in 1868 at the age of seventy-four and he is buried in Baldhu churchyard where his wife, Joey, was buried four years earlier. He had the distinction of being a Bible Christian local preacher for forty-three years.

Billy Bray's 'Three Eyes' Chapel, Kerley Downs

Billy Bray's obelisk, Baldhu churchyard.

Blackwater

Blackwater Literary Institute – Gift of a local benefactor

The Literary Institute of Blackwater, near Truro earns a place in this book for two reasons. Firstly because it is quintessential of the Victorian conception of design for small public buildings, and secondly because it is there through the generosity of a local benefactor with a remarkable history – a local lad who 'made good' and who was known as the Carnegie of Cornwall.

John Passmore Edwards was born of humble parentage in Blackwater and this particular building is among the dozens of libraries, schools, orphanages and hospitals which he gave to Cornwall, Devon and London.

Edwards was born in 1823 and lived to the age of eighty-eight. His father, William, had several jobs during his lifetime, including that of carpenter, brewer and market gardener. It is said that the cottage in which the family lived had more rooms than windows because of the infamous window tax of the time.

Educational opportunities in Cornwall at that time were almost non-existent but William Edwards passed on to his four sons a thirst for knowledge. He was the only person in Blackwater who bought the *Penny Magazine*, a London periodical, and by the age of ten John perused this very assiduously each time a new edition entered the house. His desire for knowledge and books knew no bounds and by saving a few shillings from his meagre wages (earned by helping his father in the family market garden) he was able to purchase a few books to start his own library.

In early adulthood he started, with the help of his friend John Symons, a free school in Blackwater and taught men and boys how to read and write. Edwards and Symons (who later became a builder and ran his own firm) had attended Wesleyan Sunday School together in Blackwater and John Edwards aspired to break into the literary world. He had a burning desire to improve not only his own, but also the lives of all working people.

In the 1840s he began to work for a Truro lawyer, but his biographer, R.S. Best, tells us that as John was leaving work one day he met a representative of the *Sentinel*, a London newspaper, who offered him the job of business agent for the newspaper in Manchester; this was to be the beginning of a wonderful life of success and philanthropy. He had achieved his ambition of being in journalism, but starting was not easy. Before success came, Edwards had become bankrupt and his health had deteriorated, but he was undaunted. He was an avid campaigner against drugs, alcohol and gambling, and he became a successful and wealthy newspaper owner. He was also elected Liberal MP for Salisbury, but he did not enjoy political life and soon left it.

Between 1899 and 1904 he paid for the construction of almost fifty buildings in London, Essex and the south coast, and twenty buildings in his native Cornwall.

Blackwater Literary Institute.

One of the first places to benefit was his home village of Blackwater. Following a request from the vicar of Mithian for a few books for the parishioners, John Edwards promptly gave 500 volumes and provided money for the building of the Blackwater Literary Institute in 1889, situated within 100yds of his former family home. In all he provided no less that sixty-four buildings with the aim of assisting the education and wellbeing of working people.

The Blackwater Literary Institute was built by Symons. The land for the Institute was given by Lord Falmouth and the stone for it was given by the Lords of the Manor of Tywarnhayle. The masonry was done by James Orowse & Son and it was designed by Solomon & Co. It cost £260, which included the furnishings. A stone over the door is inscribed: 'This building was erected by John Passmore Edwards Esq. of London and presented to the inhabitants of Blackwater, his native village. 1889-1900'.

Over the years the building has deteriorated and today the residents of Blackwater are seeking to renovate it and bring it back to its former glory as the village currently has no village hall. Various funding sources are being investigated and there is great support from the villagers, including young people. Mr Dean Evans is an enthusiastic campaigner for the restoration and steering has been formed to take the project forward.

BODMIN

Tower Hill Farmhouse – Perkin Warbeck was here

Tucked away in a side road almost in the centre of busy Bodmin is one of the town's oldest and most interesting buildings. It was probably built in the fourteenth century, although the stone in the wall has a date of 1641. It is the oldest surviving house in Bodmin and has possible links with the priory in the town. The house, farmyard and walled garden have not changed much, but the town has grown up around them, taking in what were once the farm's fields.

In the early seventeenth century the house was owned by John Hoblyn, and his family remained the owners until 1794 when Thomas Mudge established his tanyard nearby and purchased the house. It is likely that the family had only recently moved to the town as the Cornwall Protestation Returns of 1641 does not list any Mudge for the Bodmin parish. The Mudge family have owned Tower Hill Farmhouse ever since, the current owner being Mr Richard Mudge, who inherited it in 1991.

The present owner's great grandfather, a surgeon, had a single-storey annexe built for use as a surgery in the early nineteenth century, and during that time the house was regarded as a gentleman's residence. Another room in the house was used as the manorial courtroom during John Hoblyn's ownership in the early seventeenth century, and a relic of this is an original Tudor Rose motif in plaster on the ceiling of that room.

The house had served as a vicarage before the present one was build in 1768 and there are local stories (so far unsubstantiated) of tunnels leading from the house and its environs to the church and priory. Annual Corporation functions were held there during the occupancy of the early Mudges, two of whom were mayors in the town.

Perkin Warbeck, pretender to the throne of Henry VII, is reputed to have been entertained at the house in 1497. Warbeck made a final attempt on his goal with some followers in Cornwall, some of whom could have been the family living at Tower Hill at the time. Warbeck was captured some time afterwards and was hanged in the Tower of London.

Tower Hill is today a private residence, but the exterior can be viewed from the public road. The interior is fascinating, with original closely-set slate slabs on the bare earth flooring of the kitchen and pilasters to the wide fire recess also of slate. Hitherto hidden Tudor mouldings have been uncovered on the door jamb and there may be more treasures to be revealed as the lengthy restoration continues.

Bodmin Jail – A place of memories

If you want to be spooked you must visit Bodmin Jail! It is an extraordinary Victorian building with lots of atmosphere. It is constructed in local stone which, we are told by local historian Peter Davis, was quarried in the immediate vicinity. The gatehouse is deceptive, it is imposing and quite architecturally pleasing, but once through it the scene changes and there is nothing benign about it because the gatehouse leads into the yard where public hangings took place and attracted large crowds of onlookers in days gone by.

The jail was the first to be built in accordance with the ideas of reformer John Howard, whose concept it was to house prisoners in individual cells. It was, however, notorious for its cramped conditions and public hangings and people came from miles around to witness the latter 'spectacle'. Howard also approved of the building being of local stone as it gave the building a slightly warmer appearance than harder grey stone.

The jail housed both male and female prisoners and they were provided with clothes of more superior quality than those supplied in many other jails in the country. The prisoners were also given employment to keep them occupied and keep their spirits up in accordance with Howard's humanitarian ideals. Basic education was available for those who needed it and health was monitored on a scale appropriate to the times. Therefore, all in all, the prisoners, although often serving harsh sentences, experienced 'luxuries' that were far in advance of the times when compared to other such institutions.

For many inmates, however, such as the mentally deranged or the very dregs of society who could not appreciate the 'comforts' on offer, there was little compassion and many left after serving their sentence in as distressed a state as they were when they were charged.

The original jail building was abandoned in the 1850s and much of what remains today dates from after that time. The civil prison closed in 1918 but the Admiralty operated its section as a Navy prison until 1922. Nowadays its high, stark walls and barred windows overlooking a grassed area which was presumably once an exercise yard, still has the ability to send a shiver down your spine. Look long enough and you will imagine you see faces at those blank, barred windows – it's eerie!

In 1929 all the buildings were sold and part of the jail has, in more recent years, operated as a nightclub and then as a museum. The museum includes incredibly lifelike figures forming a tableaux occupying various cells, criminals portrayed and their crimes listed.

Bodmin Jail. (Courtesy of Dr Bill Johnson)

BUDE

The Castle – The house on sand

The Castle certainly looks the part, even if it is on the smallish side when compared to most baronial 'piles'. It was the creation and home of a remarkable man whose ingenuity and inventive expertise was without bounds: Sir Goldsworthy Gurney. He was born at Treator, near Padstow, in 1793. From an early age he showed tendencies to brilliance, as well as an interest in steam locomotion, and he later became friends with Cornish engineer Richard Trevithick, which further fuelled his enthusiasm. He put his interest to good use by working on, and discovering, the principle of the steam jet, which was adopted by George Stephenson for his famous steam locomotive *Rocket*.

Gurney himself used his discovery in pioneering work in a diversity of projects, such as blast furnaces, coal-mine ventilation and marine engineering. He was also keenly interested in, and helped to develop, the electric telegraph.

Most cars may now be considered either the greatest boon ever known to mankind or something better never invented, but, like them or loathe them, motor cars owe a lot to the inventive genius of Goldsworthy Gurney. He actually made one of the first mechanically-

Bude Castle. (Courtesy of Gerald Fry)

powered vehicles to run on British roads as early as 1839 and drove what was possibly the earliest model from London to Bath and back. But, the world was not yet ready for the motor car; horse power still reigned supreme and Gurney, probably disillusioned, abandoned his experiments with early cars.

In 1832 he acquired a ground lease from Sir J.D. Acland in Bude and immediately set about building a unique home on it. The site was not ideal for the purpose as it was part of the great sand dunes known as West Shalder, but nothing daunted Gurney and he excavated and constructed a flat concrete base, with the help of rocks beneath the sand, dispensing with traditional foundations. It was revolutionary, but it worked.

Gurney called his new home 'The Castle'. The Tithe Apportionment of 1840 described The Castle as 'a house, lawns and pleasure garden in a little more than two acres of land.' Subsequent owners made alterations to the building, but the general scale and outline of the front is very similar to the original. Gurney's expertise as an engineer had paid off because today The Castle is still standing as sturdy as ever. Gurney went on to invent a veritable myriad of useful and unique benefits to mankind and his house was the first place lighted by his Bude Light, where a stream of oxygen was introduced to the flame of an oil lamp to produce an intense light suitable for lighthouses and later adopted to light the Houses of Parliament. Who needed electricity when they had the Bude Light?

In 1850, Sir Goldsworthy gave up The Castle and lived at Hornacott Manor at Boyton and Reeds at Poughill, dying there on 28 February 1876.

The house on sand is now the venue for educational activities and various events are held in the grounds.

Penfound – The oldest manor and a Civil War ghost

One of the historical and architectural gems of north Cornwall is Penfound Manor near Bude – and it harbours a grisly legend. Its entry in the Domesday Book may need a little explanation these days as it uses words which have all dropped out of our language today. When the Domesday Book was compiled, Briend the Saxon held four manors in the area, including Penfound. The Domesday Book refers to 'part geld for half a virgate of land' at Penfound, and the manor's holdings included 'one plough, one serf and two bordars and two acres of meadow'. Geld was the tax paid by landowners to the Crown under Saxon and early Norman kings, and virgate was an old measure of land. A serf was a feudal labourer attached to an estate, and a bordar was a feudal serf of the lowest rank, doing manual work in return for a cottage which he held at his master's will.

Penfound Manor, Bude.

Penfound claims to be the oldest manor in the country; 'Penfou' meant 'head of the stream' and the manor had several different spellings before it finally became 'Penfound' in 1578.

The house was considerably extended over the centuries and the original would have borne little resemblance to what we see today. It would have been far smaller than it is now; being in Saxon and Norman times just a great hall, with a fire space in the centre with the smoke going through an aperture in the roof. Today only the north and west walls of the original building remain and they are 6ft thick, so no wonder they have stood the test of time.

In 1589 the main staircase was built along with the solar (a room constructed to enjoy the best of the sun). The solar is known as the Haunted Room. Legend has it that during the Civil War the room was Kate Penfound's bedroom. She was in love with John Trebarfoot of Trebarfoot Manor, a few miles away, but the Penfounds did not regard it as a suitable match and when Kate tried to elope with her lover, her father, Nicholas Penfound, heard her climbing down the ladder from her room and went out with a drawn sword, slaying both the lovers. In the melee which ensued Nicholas was himself killed. Kate is now said to wander around the manor, her ghost always disappearing at the head of the main staircase.

The house is privately owned and is not open to the public. The Penfound family lived there for several hundred years but there are no Penfounds there now.

calstock

The Prospect Tower – A mystery building

In the fields on the Cotehele estate, to the north of the house, stands a curious building the purpose of which has never been determined. The origin of this strange three-sided tower will probably always remain a mystery. It is approximately 30ft tall and constructed of local stone, with rough granite pinnacles and pointed dummy windows. It is three storeys high and originally there was no staircase as it was hollow and roofless. A few socket holes which survived inside the wall suggested that there may once have been a wooden stairway with an identifiable, but long-blocked, staircase entrance. In 1890, the National Trust, which owns the Cotehele estate, constructed a stair and it is now possible to ascend the tower and experience the fine view from the top, hence its name.

The tower has one unusual architectural feature which both intrigues and baffles specialists: the walls are dished on each of the three sides, the slight concavity creating a clever optical illusion. From a distance the tower could be mistaken for a church tower, but it certainly is not that.

The local legend is that is was built to enable the Edgecumbe family at Cotehele to signal from it to Maker Church, eleven miles distant as the crow flies. It is believed that when the Edgecumbe family was moving from Cotehele to Mount Edgecumbe, or vice versa, it may have been used to signal servants at either house to prepare for the family's arrival, but whether this is true or not has never been verified.

Another theory was that it was a folly, as most country estates could boast of such structures which were highly fashionable in the late eighteenth and early nineteenth centuries. This idea was given credence when it was later discovered that on a visit by King George III and Queen Charlotte to Cotehele in 1789, members of the Edgecumbe family spoke of an intention to construct obelisks and arches on the property to commemorate the Royal visit. There are no traces of any other buildings on the estate, but the tower may have been the first part of a plan which never fully came to fruition. There is, however, a folly in the grounds of Mount Edgecumbe gardens, overlooking Plymouth Sound. Prospect Tower is part of the National Trust's Cotehele Estate and visitors to the National Trust property can include the tower in their visit if they are prepared for a short walk away from the house to get to it.

Camelford

Warmington House – A town house with a ghost

In a quiet road running at the back of the busy main street of Camelford is a large and imposing townhouse which is currently being restored. Warmington House dates from the early 1600s but has been extensively altered over the years and as it stands today is totally Georgian, as can be seen from the façade.

The house, which is Grade II listed, has certainly had its ups and downs over the centuries. It was sold to George Warmington, from whom it takes its name, in the early eighteenth century for the sum of £190. In 1720 Lord Falmouth bought it and in 1822 it was sold to the Earl of Darlington, who later became the Duke of Cleveland. The Duke, however, bought the property purely as an investment and had no intention of living there. Included in the deal with Darlington was a pew in the parish church of Lanteglos-by-Camelford.

In 1879 it became the home of Sir James Smith who founded the well known, and still very much flourishing, Sir James Smith Grammar School in the town. On his demise demand for such a large house in a small town was not great and the building became the Darlington Hotel, taking its name from its earlier owner.

Dimitri and Sarah, who are currently restoring Warmington House, Camelford.

The house is built of stone and cob. The only granite in it is the lintel of the large fireplace in the main downstairs room; this is surprising in view of the town's proximity to the granite quarries of Bodmin Moor and granite being almost 'a local commodity'. The wooden flooring comprises planks 14ft wide and the building has twenty-two rooms, albeit some of them very small, but ideally suited for hotel purposes. Incidentally, during restoration some massive A-frame beams have been uncovered, having been hidden by a plaster ceiling.

The house is reputedly haunted, but by 'a nice spirit' according to those who have encountered it. Legend has it that the spirit is that of Thomas Robert John, who is buried in the nearby Methodist Chapel graveyard, and that the spectre is still present in the house. It must be admitted that some rooms do feel eerily cold and in one room it is impossible to take a clear photograph in it. That room is said to have once been the housekeeper's retreat and in it objects have been known to have moved from their original positions — maybe the housekeeper is still hard at work.

The house has a steep garden at the back and those who reach the summit are rewarded with far-reaching views over the town of Camelford and Bodmin Moor.

The picturesque Marydazy Pool, Bodmin Moor.

come-to-good

The Friends' Meeting House – A Quaker place of worship

This is a charming little thatched building in a peaceful setting among trees, and it is said to be the oldest Quaker meeting house in England.

The Friends' Meeting House at Come-to-Good, south of Truro, was built in 1710 of cob. Cob is formed of clay and straw and was a very popular material at the time in Cornwall and Devon, being very warm in the winter and cool in the summer. It is claimed that there are only three buildings like this in the country, and its burial ground is even older than the building.

In keeping with the Quaker way of life it is unadorned and totally unpretentious. Its seating is simple plain benches, although it does boast a gallery. It has old-fashioned lattice windows and shutters and a mounting stone outside for the convenience of worshippers who travelled to it on horseback. It also has an open shelter for horses and traps or jingles to be parked while the owners are attending the services.

Come-to-Good Quaker Meeting House, dating from the eighteenth century.

The Religious Society of Friends – or Quakers as they are more commonly known – have a long and distinguished connection with Cornwall. George Fox, the leader and organiser of the Friends movement, came to Cornwall during the Civil War and was promptly arrested, but many of the good people of Falmouth visited him, respected and accepted his views and he sowed the seeds of the Quaker community in the county. By 1660 regular meetings were being held. George was imprisoned in Doomsdale in Launceston Castle, a terrible place of incarceration, but the Quakers still flourished in Cornwall.

George Fox must not be confused with the Fox family who created the beautiful gardens of Trebah, Glendurgan and Penjerrick. Although the wealthy family were devout Quakers they came from Fowey to Falmouth in about 1762 and were not related to George Fox.

falmouth

Pendennis & St Mawes Castles – Henry VIII's defences

Cornwall is rich in castles and by the time of Henry VIII the style and pattern of such edifices had considerably changed, as may be seen in the handsome and forbidding Pendennis and the smaller St Mawes Castles. The buildings remind one of Henry VIII himself: solid, well built, almost rotund, and very powerful.

These two castles have to be taken in tandem because they both serve the same purpose: they were part of Henry VIII's scheme to defend the south coast of England. They are strategically placed facing each other across the Carrick Roads.

During the 1530s, Henry's attempts to get rid of his first wife Catherine of Aragon when he fell under the spell of Anne Boleyn, infuriated Emperor Charles V, ruler of Spain, the Netherlands and Germany. Pope Paul III also disapproved of Henry's antics and Francis I of France joined forces with Emperor Charles in the fight against England. Henry responded with a hectic programme of coastal defences in the 1530s and '40s, and this included building new castles and blockhouses.

Pendennis Castle, Falmouth.

St Mawes Castle, Falmouth.

Henry had already built small blockhouses at Pendennis and St Mawes in an attempt to prevent French ships and pirates entering the river Fal, and their remains can still be seen close to the castles. Henry, however, decided something more substantial and menacing was needed and so, in 1539, he ordered work to begin on Pendennis Castle. Once that castle was almost complete work started on St Mawes in 1540. Both were completed by 1543.

Both these castles could be described as revolutionary in design; they were based on typical German military plans, with Henry employing a German military architect in 1530. Henry's castles were purely and simply constructed to fight off invaders; they were not designed, as the earlier Cornish castles were, as places of residence and administration. They were defences and nothing else, furnished with heavy guns and plenty of soldiers to hold them against the enemy. They were built round in shape – the idea being to make them a difficult target from the sea.

Pendennis stands on the western promontory overlooking the entrance to the river Fal and St Mawes is close to the water, with a protecting hill behind it. When you are close to them it is easy to see how very effective they must have been in their purpose.

St Mawes Castle is smaller than Pendennis and one could say that it is slightly more artistic, having Latin inscriptions on its outer wall. However, it also has its darker side, as illustrated by

St Mawes Castle from the sea.

the 'murder hole' just inside the entrance, a lethal trap for any intruder; whether it actually caught any is not known. Men and guns lived in close proximity and the only domestic offices was the kitchen at the base of the keep. When fully manned St Mawes had a complement of 100 soldiers.

Members of the well-known Cornish family of Vyvyan were governors of the castle until 1630 and they must have endured pretty grim and Spartan conditions despite their important position. When Hannibal Vyvyan warned Sir Francis Drake of the approach of the Spanish ships, Queen Elizabeth I was so grateful that in 1600 she presented the castle with a bell inscribed with the governor's name.

During the Civil War the governor of St Mawes Castle was Hannible Bonython, who, in 1646, surrendered the castle to the Parliamentarians without a fight. This was the only action in which the castle of St Mawes was ever involved.

Until 1920 the castle was manned as part of a coastal defence scheme and at the outbreak of the Second World War was again put on a war footing. Since 1946, however, it has been a public amenity overseen by English Heritage and much enjoyed by members of the public who can wander around the building. Pendennis Castle is also open to the public.

feock

Trelissick – The water tower

Visitors to the beautiful gardens of the National Trust's Trelissick estate not far from Truro, in the parish which is the official home of the Bishop of Truro, are often intrigued by the distinctive massive round tower which is almost the first thing they see as they enter the property. It looks like the detached part of a former medieval castle and the Gothic-shaped small windows add to the illusion – you can almost imagine arrows being shot from it. But a castle it was not – far from it in fact. The tower was actually built in about 1865 and this extraordinary edifice, believe it or not, was a water tower.

Before a reservoir was built to serve Trelissick, the tower provided water for the whole estate. The crucial construction point of the building was the height of the tower, because it gave a good head of water for fire fighting. In the steeply pointed roof was a bell which was rung to mark working hours for the estate staff and it also doubled as a fire alarm. There is a narrow spiral staircase with fifty stairs in the tower and in times of emergency the person responsible for ringing the alarm bell would have to have been very fleet of foot.

The added surprise is that the National Trust has now converted this unique building into holiday accommodation, but one needs to be fairly active to be able to enjoy its interior comforts. The narrow spiral staircase leads to just one small circular room on each floor: on the first floor there is one bedroom; on the second floor a sitting room and on the third floor is a kitchen-cum-diner. The bathroom is on the ground floor and accessed by its own outside door under the porch.

One would need to be quite dedicated and enjoy unusual buildings to choose to spend a holiday in a water tower, but it would be quite a talking point for when you got home, and the setting is idyllic.

The Water Tower, Trelissick, Feock.

gunwalloe and tewaillian

Two distinctive inns

'Cornwall is awash with character pubs' claimed an enthusiastic travel writer in an American magazine several years ago. Although this may have been something of an exaggeration, Cornwall certainly does have some very distinctive inns. Two in particular are Halzephron Inn at Gunwalloe and The Wheel Inn at Tresillian.

The Halzephron is in the small village of Gunwalloe, near Helston, and it is a sixteenth-century building which has traded as an inn almost since that time. The strange name (which some people find quite hard to pronounce) is from a phrase in the old Cornish language which translates as 'cliffs of hell'. The name is very appropriate for its location because the high and dangerous cliffs with their tide-washed caves were ideal for those intent on smuggling.

In the sixteenth, seventeenth and eighteenth centuries smuggling was rife in Cornwall and in those days was almost regarded as a normal occupation, provided you didn't get caught. The Halzephron has what is known locally as a 'smugglers' tunnel', which runs from the attic down through the building and underneath the road outside to emerge in the nearby treacherous cliffs, which are said to have been the haunt of smugglers and wreckers of long ago. These unpleasant characters, according to old Cornish traditional tales, used to stand on the cliff waving lanterns to lure sailing ships on to the lethal rocks. Once the ship foundered

The Wheel Inn, Tresillion.

the wreckers would plunder the cargo with little respect for human life and leave the stricken sailors to their watery doom. In recent years this story has been refuted, but is believed by most old Cornish people, so one must assume there is a grain of truth in it.

The lovely old inn has won many awards in modern times, has also been most favourably mentioned in prestigious gastronomic guides and has been featured on television. It is a delightful old building and its fascinating history attracts custom from all over the world.

The Wheel Inn at Tresillian abuts the main road near Truro and is famous for another distinctive feature. It is one of the best-known and picturesque public houses in the county. It is an ancient building with a beautiful thatched roof and pretty small-paned windows. Its 'trademark' which attracts so much attention is the large straw wheel which adorns its roof. The large cartwheel is a superb example of the thatcher's 'alternative' skill, because not only does a skilled thatcher thatch roofs, he also makes decorative objects in straw, such as birds, fish, and, in this case, a wheel to decorate that lovely thatched roof. It is an eye-catcher and naturally attracts a lot of passing trade in additional to the large local clientele. It is certainly distinctive.

helston

Bochym – One of the oldest houses in Cornwall

Bochym Manor is one of the oldest houses in Cornwall. Goonhilly Downs is now famous for the telecommunications satellite-tracking station with its massive dish aerials, but the area was once one of the most remote parts of the British Isles, and at the very edge of these desolate downs was the valley of Bochym. Bochym has been inhabited for at least 2,500 years and possibly by Stone-Age man before that.

In the Domesday survey of 1086 it was recorded that Robert of Mortain, half brother of William the Conqueror, held among all his land in Cornwall the manor of Bochym, called in the survey 'Buchent', so it is little wonder that the name of Bochym has a French sound to it.

Bochym Manor, Helston.

By the end of the thirteenth century things had changed and the estate was in the hands of the Catholic family of Le Bret, who, in 1408, built a chapel dedicated to the Blessed Virgin Mary in the parish of Cury.

In the late fifteenth century the great heiress the Lady Marina inherited Bochym, whom, after her marriage to Richard Winslade Esquire, joined her estate to his. After her death in 1504 it passed to her son William, who in turn left it to his eldest son John Winslade.

John Winslade, however, was not a lucky man and in those uncertain times he became a ringleader in the upheaval of the Cornish Prayer Book Rebellion, a move which cost him his life as he was beheaded and all his land was forfeited to the Crown, to be eventually divided up between Sir Peter Carew and Sir Reginald Mohyn, with the latter being given the manor of Bochym.

During the Civil War Bochym was a Royalist stronghold and as such was burnt down by Cromwell's army, but it was rebuilt over a period of nearly forty years by Christopher Bellot, who had become a relative of Mohyn through marriage. The stone in the wall of the present north window, commemorating the completion of the rebuilding, was put there by Mohyn's son, Renatus. Terraced gardens and a bowling green were also added at that time.

The ambitious rebuilding created a big hole in the family fortunes and in 1712 the estate was sold to George Robinson of Nansloe in Wendron parish to settle debts, and his family later sold it to the Trelawney family. Sir Harry Trelawney later passed it to his son William, who in turn sold it to Robert Furneaux, the designer of the first Lizard Lighthouse.

The house was later acquired by a man who spent nothing whatsoever on its upkeep and it fell into serious disrepair until being bough in 1825 by Stephen Davey, who had made a fortune through tin mining. He restored the manor to its former glory and this author's mother, born in 1878, always remembered being entertained there as a small child with her parents, saying a visit to Squire Davey was always an occasion for wearing best clothes. Mr Davey added another wing to the house and made other embellishments to the estate, including improving the gardens, which were laid out and planted with many exotic trees and shrubs, and the estate 'came to life again'.

During the 1851 rebuilding, a secret passage was discovered in the wall running from the north wing. It is believed to have led to Mullion and been used extensively by smugglers.

The Davey family remained at Bochym until the death of Joshua Sidney Davey in 1909, when it passed, by the marriage of his daughter, to the Lee family from whom it was bought in 1974 by the present owner, who has made many improvements to modernise the living accommodation.

A real curiosity in the grounds is a mulberry tree in the garden at the front of the house; it is reputed to be the oldest mulberry tree in the country.

The house has been open to the public and enquiries should be made concerning public access today. It is an exciting place to visit and has great atmosphere.

Trelowarren – Home of a family with very ancient origins

The name of Vyvyan has been synonymous with Cornwall for many centuries. They have lived on the site of Trelowarren since the year 1427 and have been prominent in Cornish public life for almost as long. The Vyvyans have records covering the 500 years of the family at Trelowarren.

The first known owner of Trelowarren, recorded in the Domesday Book, is Earl Harold who died at the Battle of Hastings in 1066, and in 1086 the property passed into the hands of Robert of Mortain, half brother of William the Conquerer.

The earliest recorded ancestor of the Vyvyans is one Vivian, whose son, Ralph of Trevidran, St Buryan, is mentioned in the Patent Rolls of 1212. The family history tells us that in the

Trelowarren House and chapel, Helston.

same century there is the record of a Sir Vyell Vyvyan who married Margaret, a daughter of Christopher, Earl of Kildare.

It must be admitted that the early Vyvyan ancestors appear to have seen something of a 'rip roaring' family going their own way and doing their own thing, doubtless to the grave concern of those in authority. In 1328 the Bishop of Exeter excommunicated Richard Vyvyan and his sons, William and Hugh, along with other men of St Buryan after they had assaulted the rector of St Just in Penwith in his churchyard. In 1331, Richard Vyvyan was indicted for carrying away merchandise adjudged to be a wreck, and in 1334 his sons were accused of assaulting John de Lanbrun at Helston. But things did get better. In 1398, Adam Vyvyan was pardoned for lying in wait and murdering John Nicol at Bodmin on Easter Day, and in 1389 Ralph and Thomas were pardoned for having slain John Trebuer at Mousehole. This record of lawlessness takes some beating.

However, later generations of the Vyvyans did not follow the early trend and the family became extremely respectable and important, renowned for their good works. In the early sixteenth century Thomas Vyvyan was prior of Bodmin and titular Bishop of Megara, and he is buried in a very impressive tomb in St Patroc's Church in Bodmin . A long succession of Vyvyans were captains of Pendennis Castle and during the Civil War the family was staunchly Royalist.

King Charles I was said to have stayed at Trelowarren and after the Civil War various alterations and improvements were made to the house. A room at Trelowarren is known as the King Charles' room and he is believed to have stayed in it.

There have been many alterations to Trelowarren over the years and although the outside remains Elizabethan in style, the interior is Victorian. The alterations were beautifully done and Trelowarren is now a very dignified and interesting property. It is now open to the public and members of the Vyvyan family still live in the north wing. The delightfully light and intimate chapel is now leased to Trelowarren Fellowship, an ecumenical charity which is also responsible for the maintenance of the 1662 wing. All in all it is a most intriguing property with a colourful history.

Godolphin – A National Trust acquisition

As Cornish estates go, Godolphin came out top of the pile in the seventeenth century when the house was regarded as the largest and grandest in the county. John Godolphin built the house in 1475 on the site of a fourteenth-century castle erected by Sir Alexander Godolphin, and over the centuries it developed into that degree of grandeur which made it stand out.

One of the great treasures of the house is the outstandingly magnificent linenfold panelling which line the dining room.

The Godolphins were immensely wealthy and powerful, with most of their money accumulated through mining, indeed their home was situated in the centre of the richest mining area in Cornwall. The wealth and importance of the family was demonstrated by the fact that, although the house was far from the fashionable centres of Europe, it was still visited by Royalty as well as leading figures in every aspect of cultural life. The King's Room in the house (formerly the Great Chamber) was named in honour of King Charles II, who stayed at Godolphin in 1646 on his escape to France, and a portrait of him hangs in the room.

By 1785 there were no Godolphin heirs and the estate passed through the second Earl of Godolphin's daughter to the Dukes of Leeds, whose seat was in Yorkshire. They planned to extend the house, but the grandiose ideas never came to fruition and they became merely absentee landlords, investing very little in the estate but extracting considerable amounts of money from its mining and farming interests.

In 1910 the estate was sold by the then Duke of Leeds and the house was used as a farmhouse. It was a sad downfall from the glory days and it became derelict and was not lived in again until it was acquired by the Schofield family in 1937, after which it remained a working farm until 1999.

Over the years the house was patched up, but by 1991 it was in need of major repair. In December 1999 a lifeline was thrown when the National Trust purchased the estate for

Godolphin House, Helston.

preservation in perpetuity, whilst the Schofield family retained private ownership of the house, and thus began a unique partnership.

The partnership had great benefits in attracting allocations from English Heritage, which meant that the major repairs would be carried out in several phases. It was stressed that the house was being repaired and not restored and the difference is important: the old features would be retained, but where they were beyond repair they would be replaced. For example, in the entrance hall the floor was laid with lime pavers actually made at Godolphin, using lime from Gynwalloe not very far away. This is not strictly authentic but it allows the floor to now 'breathe' and was decided upon only after careful consideration and research.

Since the National Trust's involvement both the house and the estate have been the setting for a number of cultural events extolling the Cornish way of life and the wealth of artistic talent in the county. The National Trust has been responsible for the 550 acres of the estate, providing great walking and horse riding opportunities for the general public, while the Schofield family retain the 49 acre 'core', including the house, stables, farm buildings and garden. The house was open to the public in the summer season and the outbuildings were even the venue for farmers' markets selling local produce.

It was always hoped that the National Trust would eventually acquire the 'core' as well as the estate grounds, thus preserving the whole of Godolphin forever. In 1997 these hopes became a reality when, in August of that year, it was announced that the National Trust had bought the house from the Schofield family. Although there was sadness in giving up ownership, the whole family was delighted that the house now belonged to the nation. The National Trust has now launched a £500,000 fundraising appeal to cover the cost of the conservation work.

Now everybody will be able to enjoy its richness and splendour, absorb the amazing history and early craftsmanship which it holds, putting them on a par with the Royal visitors of the past.

ILLOGAN

Thomas Merritt's House – Home of a Cornish composer

It was an unpretentious little semi-detached cottage in Higher Broadlane in a not particularly fashionable area of the country, but it was the home of a man revered in Cornwall for his prowess in composing carols.

The son of a miner, Thomas Merritt was born in 1863 and died in 1908 at the age of only forty-six, but is immortalised by the vast amount of music which he composed in his short life and his fame spread far beyond the boundaries of his native county.

Merritt, a self-taught chapel organist, was born with a talent which he exploited to the full, but remained ever the humble miner's son and in adult life earned a very modest, if meagre, living as a music teacher. He left school at the age of eleven when his father died and, to help support his family, he too went into the tin mine to work, but his health forced him to give this up; he was simply not strong enough for the harsh life of tin mining. It was then that he turned his hand to teaching music, although at that time there was not much demand for musical education in the mining districts of Cornwall. He also composed music.

The Cornish have a great tradition of carol singing ('curls' as they are often called in the dialect) and Merritt tapped into that love and demand for carols in a way which can only be described as inspirational. He did not confine himself to carols; he composed hymns and anthems and even a cantata, which was performed to great acclaim at Cartmel in Cumbria after the score was discovered in a second-hand bookshop in Norwich long after the composer's death.

It is for his carols that he is best known; they are sung far beyond the boundaries of his native county as Cornish miners emigrating sung them in the mines from South Africa to Australia, from America to Canada. There is an old saying that 'wherever there was a Cousin Jack (the name given to immigrant Cornish miners) there were Merritt carols being sung by some of the finest choirs in the land. His best know work was 'Hark the Glad Sound', which could bring tears to the eyes of tough miners far from home, but there were many, many more which are loved and sung to this day.

Over the years Merritt's tiny cottage birthplace was converted by being joined to the one next to it, creating a much more spacious dwelling which today bears little resemblance to Merritt's original humble abode, but it can be seen and admired by all lovers of Merritt's music because in 1989 Carn Brea Parish Council placed on the exterior front wall a beautifully carved plaque which reads 'Cornish composer Thomas Merritt 1862-1908'. It is a simple but very moving commemoration which reflects Merritt's humble background as well as his great talent.

Thomas Merritt's house, Illogan.

The plaque is conspicuously sited in the centre of the wall of the house. Surely Merritt would be amazed if he could come back and see his former home now.

Merritt is buried in the churchyard at Illogan and a granite cross stands above his grave, which had become a place of pilgrimage for very many people.

launcells

Tackbeare – Connections with a 'gentleman' smuggler

Tackbeare Manor in North Cornwall was listed in the Domesday Book as being in the ownership of Count Robert of Mortain, half brother of William the Conqueror. From as early as 1330 Tackbeare was in the ownership of the Crown, but at the beginning of the seventeenth century things changed dramatically and the freehold was granted to a member of an old south west family, one Samuel Gilbert.

For the next 400 years Tackbeare was in the ownership of only two families, but in the early nineteenth century along came a colourful character, George Harward of Newacott. Despite being of seemingly impeccable background, he was reputed to have secrets from his past which he guarded vigorously and which made him far less respectable than he appeared to be.

Harward had been a military man and was known locally as Colonel Harward, a title which he did his utmost to preserve. He expressed deep concern about the plight of soldiers coming back from the Napoleonic Wars with no work to which to go to and he was able to offer

Tackbeare Manor, Launcells.

soldiers employment through his canal-building scheme. The canal age was still in its infancy at that time, but Harward invested in the new Bude Canal, which was designed to bring mineral rich sand from Bude to act as a fertiliser of the poor quality fields of the hinterland.

However, Harward had an even greater interest in Tackbeare than the plans for the canal. He was reputed to have been involved with smuggling in quite a big way, a practice then rife on the north Cornish coast. Harward knew that there was extensive woodland on the Tackbeare estate, an ideal hiding place for smuggled cargoes prior to distribution. It was said that cargoes were landed at not far distant Millook and Widemouth and transported to Tackbeare by mule train. Harward's cloak of respectability was said to overshadow his more nefarious activities.

The interior of the house at Tackbeare bears many reminders of its illustrious past. The present house is a Grade II listed Elizabethan manor house built on the typical pattern of the day of a central block and two wings. Ceilings in some of the main rooms have beautiful plaster mouldings dating from the seventeenth and eighteenth centuries; one depicts the Tudor Rose and all reflected the Royalist and Jacobean sympathies of the early owners.

Tackbeare has changed hands several times over the years and was most recently the home of a local faming family who ran the estate as a working farm. It is today in private ownership and not open to the public.

launceston

Launceston Castle – '1066 and all that'

For every true Cornish man and woman returning to Cornwall after a spell away from the county the sight of Launceston Castle towering above 'the town on a hill' is a heart-warming experience as one travels along the busy A30 spine road through Cornwall. It signifies 'home again'.

It stands as proud today as it did in the early years of the Norman Conquest – the reminder to everyone of the authority of the Earls (later Dukes) of Cornwall. They called it Castle Terrible; it probably was pretty grim in its day, but those were grim times. However, we are reminded by the historians that is has never fired a shot in anger. The stone keep is as dominant as ever, the gatehouses north and south are ruinous, but they are still slightly intimidating for wrongdoers. Some lengths of curtain wall still remain, as do the foundations of the Great Hall and the ruins of various domestic buildings. Together they show what a powerful and important place it must have been. The north gate is not the original but dates from the thirteenth century.

The first reference to Launceston Castle is in the Domesday Book, which records that 'the Count has one manor which is called Dunhevet'. The original name for Launceston was

Launceston Castle.

Dunheved and the Count mentioned was Robert, Count of Mortain, half brother of William the Conqueror and one of his strongest supporters in the invasion of England.

Robert was rewarded for his loyalty and trustworthiness with the Earldom of Cornwall and no less than 247 manors in the country. He was at the time one of the most powerful men in the kingdom – and he knew it!

Robert chose Launceston as the venue for the administrative centre of his kingdom and he established his court there. Dunheved was of great strategic importance and the castle controlled the whole of the county between Bodmin Moor and Dartmoor, a vast expanse in those days when there was no speedy means of travel.

It was in Robert's time that Launceston as a town was established and was, until 1840, the centre of Cornish government, with the county assizes and county jail there. Prior to that St Stephens, north of the town, was the main centre, and there is an age-old saying that 'St Stephens was a market town when Launceston was a fuzzy down' ('fuzz' being a Cornish term for gorse).

A rebellion of Count Robert's son caused the Earldom to pass out of the Mortain family when in 1106 it was forfeited to the Crown. This upheaval resulted in the castle being granted in 1141 to Reginald de Dunstanville, one of Henry I's fourteen illegitimate children. He held it until his death in 1175, after which it was granted to John by his brother Richard I, but after John's rebellion reverted to the Crown in 1191.

Much alteration took place at this turbulent time and there was no Earl of Cornwall for the first part of the thirteenth century. In 1227 the Earldom was granted by Henry III to his younger brother Richard, who held it until 1272, and he drastically rebuilt and reorganised the castle.

After Richard of Cornwall's death his son, Edmund, made further changes by shifting the Earldom's administration to Restormel Castle, Lostwithiel; the reason for this is believed to be because it was nearer to the centre of tin production, which provided the major part of the earl's revenue. After this Launceston Castle was pretty much neglected until the accession of Edward the Black Prince in 1337. In 1341 repair work commenced and continued throughout the fourteenth century.

During the Civil War the town and castle were held for the King, but the castle was captured in 1642 and 1644 by the Parliamentarians, finally being taken by the King's General in 1646. Once again changes were made: the north gatehouse became a prison, and a pretty horrendous one at that. The gatehouse was also used as lodgings for the constable of the castle (an honorary position usually bestowed on prominent citizens). The main jail remained within the bailey and, still surviving in the castle grounds, is the pump inscribed with an eighteenth-century date, which served the prison. When the assizes were moved to Bodmin in 1840 the jail was demolished. The Duke of Northumberland, then owner of Werrington Park, was instrumental in the castle and its environs being made into a public recreation area.

During the Second World War Nissen huts in the Castle Green accommodated US Army hospital and administration offices.

The castle remains in the ownership of the Duchy of Cornwall but is administered and maintained by English Heritage. The grounds and shell keep are open to the public and there is a public path through the Castle Green, where interpretation boards beside the public path give visitors a better idea of just how the castle and its surroundings once looked. The former Victorian caretaker's cottage now houses a shop selling guidebooks and gifts.

Dockacre – the oldest house in the town

This is the oldest house in Launceston. It was built during the reign of Elizabeth I, but was extensively 'modernised' in Georgian times.

Dockacre House is reputedly haunted and is also believed to have a secret passage which, according to the late Colonel Raymond Buckeridge (former owner of Dockacre), in his booklet about the house, was thought to lead to either St Mary Magdalene Church or the Norman castle. Sadly, when a new road was constructed behind the house in the nineteenth century, the passage was blocked by the foundations, but the entrance in the cellar of the house is still negotiable for a few feet.

The Dockacre ghost has over the years manifested itself in several ways to both members of the Buckeridge family, who still live there, and their guests and visitors from time to time. The late Colonel Buckeridge could relate several cases of objects being moved from one place to another, pictures inexplicably falling from the walls and doors opening without warning, but it would appear that the ghost is mischievous and not malevolent. The ghost was the inspiration for the Revd Sabine Baring-Gould's book *John Herring*.

Since the eighteenth century two pastel portraits have hung in the dining room. They are of Nicholas Herle and his wife Elizabeth, eighteenth-century owners of the house. A barrister, Herle was a figure of influence in Launceston; he was mayor of the town in 1716 and again in 1721 and was at one time High Sheriff of Cornwall, so was obviously a man of some substance.

Elizabeth Herle died in 1714 in what can only be described as mysterious circumstances. There are conflicting versions of her death. One is that she lost her reason and her husband locked her in an upstairs room at Dockacre and starved her, starvation being at that time regarded as a cure for madness, but he overdid it and she died. The other story is that Herle shot his wife on the staircase in their home; whether accidentally or deliberately has never been recorded. One of the stairs was always reputed to be bloodstained and people still alive (including this author) can recall seeing a dark stain in the wood on one stair.

Dockacre House, Launceston. (Courtesy of John Neale)

Unfortunately, the stair treads were replaced some years ago and of course the stained tread disappeared.

To add to the mystery there is a monument to Elizabeth Herle in St Mary Magdalene Church, but it is situated behind where the organ is now located and is not easily visible to the public, although it can be seen by those determined enough to venture behind the organ. It is rather revealing in that it is inscribed 'Depart ye life 25 Dec, 1714 by starvation or other means', so there is no doubt that Elizabeth did meet an untimely and highly suspicious end.

Nicholas Herle died in Hampstead, London, in 1728. Did he have a guilty secret which caused him to leave Cornwall? We shall never know, but his ghost is still allegedly seen in the hall of the house and he has left another eerie legacy – he is reputed to have always played a flute when a death is about to occur in the household.

Herle's flute was made into a walking stick, and this has led to a superstition which has lingered into modern times: all owners of the house, on leaving it, must donate a personal walking stick. The walking sticks are all kept in a sack in an attic room in the house and it is said that if not put away in the right order they will rattle themselves into it. Among these sticks is Nicholas Herle's flute stick. Over the years the legend about the flute has changed slightly in that it is now said that if anyone hears the flute being played, it foretells a death in their own family. This old tale was firmly believed by an elderly relative of this author, who, if walking past Dockacre House, would always quicken her step to get past as soon as possible – just in case she heard the ghostly sound of the flute. The room in which the sticks are kept has a tiny window which overlooks the public road so it might just be possible to hear the flute if it is played when one is passing.

Dockacre House is not open to the public, but the exterior can be viewed from the road.

The Round House – 'Newport Town Hall'

The Round House at Newport, Launceston, has been a part of the street scene for so long that no one local takes very much notice of it, but it is of great historical importance and is a Grade II listed building.

Known locally as 'Newport Town Hall', it was built in 1829 by the then Duke of Northumberland who at the time owned Werrington Park, and the building is shown on the 1845 tithe map as 'the Election House'. When built it was referred to as the Temple of Winds, after the famous ancient structure of that name in Athens, but it soon got the nickname of Newport Town Hall and there was a good reason for that. It was originally built to cover the broken shaft of the Newport market cross, which remains there today, but it also served a

The Round House at Newport, Launceston. (Courtesy of John Neale)

very useful purpose from the years 1831 to 1859 when it was the place from which the two Members of Parliament for Newport were declared. In more recent times it has been used to proclaim such news as monarchs ascending to the throne, and their jubilees.

In a monograph by Mr Jake Jackson, curator of Lawrence House Museum in Launceston, he suggests that there is ample evidence from the early Middle Ages that Newport (once regarded as a suburb of Launceston) was governed by its own corporation elected by the inhabitants and separate from that of Launceston. He adds that the earliest mention of Newport as a borough is in the Roll of Sersin in 1337 and in the Duchy accounts of 1338, and 'the town of Newport in Launceston' is twice referred to in the Priory Rent Rolls of 1474, and there are further references in the Duchy accounts of 1502.

When the massive Augustinian priory flourished at St Thomas its canons dominated Newport, but in 1540 it was dissolved in the Dissolution of the Monasteries and the Manor of Launceston in which the Borough of Newport lay was annexed to the Crown.

Officers known as Vianders were chosen annually at the lord's manor court to act as returning officers. They supervised the election of Members of Parliament by all the inhabitants of Newport who paid 'scot and lot' (a town and parish tax levied according to the ability to pay) or who had burbage tenure (by which lands or tenements in towns or cities were held for a small yearly rent). The elections took place on the open hustings in full view of the public. The inhabitants of Newport then gathered beside the cross to cheer the victorious candidates. The glory, however, did not last long, because only three years later Newport was disenfranchised under the Reform Bill of 1831.

Sadly, when its political importance ended, the Round House was used as a builder's store and was subsequently vandalised, and was later handed over to the town council. And what of the Newport market cross in the Round House, the shaft of which now remains? It too has its historical importance because it is one of the few surviving examples of market crosses in Cornwall, but no one knows just what it was like when it was complete.

Recently, help was at hand for the Round House. In 2005 Launceston Town Council restored the building, including stripping the slate roof and replacing the timbers, and erecting gates which prevent public access and any damage to the newly-restored building and the cross. A bronze plaque giving a potted history of the building has also been attached, so the Round House is well worthy of notice.

The South Gate – 'The Dark House'

In the fourteenth century Launceston was a walled town, and parts of the original wall around the town exist to this day. Guarding the entrance to the town were three gatehouses in the wall – North Gate, West Gate and South Gate. There was no East Gate because the approach to the town was so precipitous that it could never be attacked from the east – travellers from the east had to follow the track which led them to, and through, the South Gate.

Of the three gates only the South Gate remains, the others were demolished in the early nineteenth century, but the South Gate stands strong and proud and still defies any large vehicle which tries to get through it, a situation which often caused traffic chaos in the town centre until the by-pass was constructed.

The South Gate (now known as Southgate) had a dual purpose: not only was it an entrance gate, it also served as a prison. Up until 1884 it was know as the 'Dark House', and not without reason. It is reported that as far back as 1381 two keepers were employed to guard prisoners incarcerated in the South Gate. An old document in the town archives states, '1567 – Robert Craghte and Hatie doth occupy. Kept for the use of the town.' Much later, in 1805, it was

Southgate, Launceston.

described as 'a most filthy and dilapidated place.' A keeper employed at that time made frequent applications to the Mayor of Launceston for whitewash to lighten up the place, but he always had the same reply: 'The blacker it is the better, it has more appearance of a jail that way.'

In some rooms the doors were only 4ft high and 15in wide. The upper room was the debtors' prison and the lower room was for petty offenders, felons etc. The only light came from an aperture 3ft by 9in and that was almost obscured by iron bars. Straw was scattered on the floor and presumably prisoners had to sleep on that. There was a fireplace, but no fuel was allowed; a bath tub also served as a latrine and there was no courtyard and no water. A dark place indeed, with the most appalling conditions.

Overcrowding was the order of the day: the lower room was intended to house twenty-five petty offenders at any one time and in 1827 it is recorded that five burglars were sleeping in one bed, a state of affairs which prompted some caring people to send a report to the Home Secretary requesting that he intervene in the running of the jail.

The South Gate finally ceased to be used as a prison as late as 1884 and in 1886 the Launceston Historical and Scientific Society converted it into a museum which, incidentally, contained some bizarre exhibits, including a totally black loaf of bread which was reputed to have survived the Great Fire of London. Remnants of stonework from the former Augustinian priory at Newport, Launceston, were displayed on the exterior walls and still remain there. The heavy old door of the South Gate is said to have originally been the door of the condemned cell of the old prison in what is now the castle grounds, and still serves as the entrance door to the South Gate. The steep steps up to it are believed to be the original ones.

In 1887 'The Arch', as it is known locally, was bought by Richard Peter, a former Town Clerk and member of an old and very well-known Launceston family, who had it repaired and presented it to the town to commemorate Queen Victoria's Diamond Jubilee. He also had a small arch constructed at the side to serve as a pedestrian walkway and a plaque on the wall records this.

In modern times the South Gate was leased for a number of years by Mrs Penny Harris, an internationally known artist who specialised in doing exquisite paintings on glass, using a very complicated technique that involved painting in reverse. The South Gate has been home to many art and craft exhibitions in comparatively recent times, and has also served as an art gallery for several local art organisations. It is currently a photographer's studio.

For many years a sycamore tree grew, apparently without any sustenance, from the wall of 'The Arch' and is shown in all photographs of the South Gate up to some years after the Second World War. However, it grew so large that it was feared it would severely damage the masonry and could even cause the ancient structure to collapse without warning, so it was removed, much to the regret of many of the town's inhabitants who had known it all their lives, How it managed to flourish as it did will always remain a mystery, but the South Gate was never the same again without its sycamore tree, it was an icon for the town.

Eagle House – The house built 'on a lottery'

This handsome building, an impressive Georgian house, has a colourful past. Now it is a hotel, but in olden days this mansion was situated in the most exclusive part of town.

For many years it was the home of the Dingley banking family, whose Dingley & Co. (established in 1885) and Dingley Pearse & Co. (established 1856) were later incorporated in the National Provincial Bank (established 1833). However, before the Dingleys took up residence, the house had an interesting history.

One Coryndon Carpenter was an influential figure in Launceston in the eighteenth century. He was onetime mayor of the town and involved with such public bodies as the Turnpike Trust. He also held the position of Constable of the Castle, an honorary, but prestigious, appointment. Carpenter was admired by some people, but viewed by suspicion by others. In his own estimation he was a 'high flyer', enjoying the high life and usually gaining what he wanted.

The story of Eagle House demonstrates this. The long-believed story is that Carpenter won £10,000 in a lottery and this enabled him to marry the young woman he had been courting for some time but had previously found himself financially unable to make a commitment to marriage and a fine home.

As a local dignitary in the town he had power, and it was said that he was instrumental in purloining stone form the north gatehouse of Launceston Castle – an edifice which included a gaol and a gaoler's apartments – using the stone to build Eagle House nearby, and leaving the north gate in ruins. He may have thought that as Constable of the Castle he had the right to do that, but it was actually an act of vandalism which no one condoned.

The new building was faced with fine Georgian bricks and it is thought that they were imported form Portugal, being used as ballast in sailing ships at the time. The layout included stables and a coach-house, all in brick and the design of the house was imposing; it typified Coryndon Carpenter's dream. It was topped with a statue of a figure somewhat resembling Britannia and this gave rise in much later years to a story told to children that when the figure heard St Mary's Church clock stick thirteen it would descent from its lofty perch and walk to the church.

The house was completed about 1760. Carpenter was reviled in many quarters for his desecration of the gatehouse and one assumes that he died, in 1776, a very unpopular man in the town. A memorial tablet was fixed to the north wall inside St Mary Magdalene Church and many believe that such was the vanity of the man that he had written the epitaph himself prior to his demise.

Reading the fulsome tribute today, it is easy to see how such a suspicion arose. It reads:

> Here under this stone lies the remains of Coryndon Carpenter, who was born in the year 1731. Died universally lamented on 23rd April 1776. His integrity of heart and his distinguished abilities (never prostituted to base principles) rendered him at once the ornament of society and delight of all who knew him.

One's reaction today can only be 'ouch'!

Eagle House, Launceston.

Liskeard

Stuart House – Lodging for a King

Passing through the busy town of Liskeard one cannot fail to notice the impressive slate-hung building which is Stuart House.

The building in Barras Street is believed to have stood on what is now the main road through Liskeard town for at least 500 years. However, who built it and the names of the first occupants remain a mystery. During restoration work in 1994, the discovery of a screen (rather than a wall) between a room and the cross passage, which runs from front to back, helped considerably with the dating of the building; the screen consisted of wooden uprights known, we are told, as mustins (with mouldings carved on either side into which panels were slotted), confirms that the house was built during the reign of King Henry VII, about the turn of the fourteenth century.

This is not to say that the house did not undergo alterations over the years, in fact, its fourteenth-century inhabitants would certainly not recognise it today. Extensions were added,

Stuart House, Liskeard. (Courtesy of John Neale)

plus interior architectural features. Some of the extensions have since been demolished and the property has lost much of its land. It is described in early deeds as a mansion with gardens, stables, orchard and malthouse. Although it is still possible to see that it was originally a sizeable property, all its accompanying grounds and buildings have long since disappeared. The adjacent Passmore Edwards Library was built in 1898 on land which formerly belonged to Stuart House and this would have involved demolition of part of the mansion. In much later times a large garage business took up yet more of the land.

Stuart House was still a rather grand (although small) mansion in the seventeenth century and King Charles I spent six nights in the house while he was waging his campaign against the heavily fortified town of Lostwithiel, then held by the Parliamentarians during the Civil War. From there Charles moved west to Pendennis Castle, Falmouth, where his wife Queen Henrietta Maria had sought refuge. Having assured himself of her safety, Charles returned to Stuart House for one more night before moving on to pastures new in his campaign. The chamber where he slept is still known as the King's Room and Liskeard Old Cornwall Society was instrumental in erecting a plaque on the building in commemoration of the Royal visit.

At the time of the King's visit the house was occupied by the Jane family, staunch Royalists. The first reference to the Jane family connection with the house was in 1487, so they had a very long connection with the property; presumably the house took its name from their loyalty to the house of Stuart.

The house's finest feature is the magnificent eighteenth-century staircase which rises through its three-storeys; it has a number of special features and is a classic example of the carpenters' art in those days. It bears testimony to the opulence of the dwelling in its heyday.

For lovers of the mysterious there is a tunnel or passage which goes from the cellar, underneath the staircase and for about fifty yards after that before being blocked as the result of a roof fall many years ago. Its purpose is unknown and can be as romantic of utilitarian as you care to make it. One suggestion is that it led to the cellar of a house in Fore Street, enabling the residents of Stuart House to make a quick getaway if circumstances demanded.

The much-admired slate hanging of the west front gives the impression of having been there since King Charles's time, but it is actually the work of nineteenth-century craftsmen.

The building is now owned and administered by the Stuart House Trust, formed in 1984 to purchase, restore and develop an Arts and Heritage Centre for Liskeard and south east Cornwall. The work was completed in 1999 thanks to grants from English Heritage and the National Lottery, as well as generous local fund-raising. It has facilities for art, craft and heritage exhibitions, musical recitals, poetry, plays, seminars, lectures, club meetings, fund-raising events and even coffee mornings. It is open daily from 9.30 a.m. and welcomes visitors.

the lizard

Tater Dhu – A modern lighthouse

We tend to think that lighthouses around our coast have been there almost forever, certainly from Victorian times or even earlier. However, a modern lighthouse, dating only from the 1960s, was built after tragedy struck Tater Dhu and highlighted the desperate need for a lighthouse on that particular part of the coastline.

Tater Dhu is a prominent headland between Lamorna and Porthcurno, west of Penzance, and it is here that the last lighthouse to be built in Cornwall is situated. It is in the ideal situation, overlooking a highly treacherous group of rocks.

Prior to 1965 buoys were the only warnings of the dangers of the deadly Runnelstone Rocks, where it is estimated that over thirty ships have been wrecked over the years, and it was only following a tragedy in modern times that the Tater Dhu lighthouse came into existence. It was the wreck of the Spanish ship *Juan Ferrer* off Boscawen Point in 1963 – with the loss of eleven lives – that prompted action. A fully automated light were therefore erected on a headland two miles west of Lamorna Cove.

A strongly worded request had gone to Trinity House from the Newlyn and Mousehole Fishermen's Association, asking for a light of some sort between Mousehole and Land's End, one of the most dangerous stretches of water around the Cornish coast, and the tragic loss of the *Juan Ferrer* triggered an almost instant reaction to local demand.

At first a small local light was considered, but it was finally decided that a light and fog horn powerful enough to be helpful to all shipping and not just for vessels using local harbours was needed, so construction of the Tater Dhu lighthouse began. It was completed within a period of eighteen months and is certainly different from the traditional lighthouse design. It is built of white concrete blocks with a 45ft tower of unconventional design created by Humphreys Ltd of Knightsbridge, London. It is fully automated so no lighthouse keepers are needed. It was opened on 17 July 1965 by the then master of Trinity House, the Duke of Gloucester, and was further modernised in 1966 and 1967, and was remotely controlled from Penzance.

The light is switched on and off by a time switch with a solar dial device and is monitored by Trinity House. The light has a range of approximately twenty-three miles in clear weather, reducing to approximately eighteen miles in adverse conditions. The light is actually equal to 300,000 candle power: a rather staggering figure when one stops to think of the power of the beams in early lighthouses.

The Tater Dhu lighthouse.

The fog signal has seventy-two loudspeaker units, looking from the exterior like a patterned grid in the tower wall. A separate light some 10ft down from the top of the tower shines a fixed red light over the Runnelstone to the west.

It is a remarkably ingenious structure using modern technology at its best. The design is pleasing to the eye and fits into the landscape; a twentieth-century lighthouse and a very commendable example of modern design with the architect seriously taking into consideration its natural location.

Lostwithiel

Taprell House – Now a literary haven

Visiting the library in Lostwithiel has special significance because it is situated in one of the oldest buildings in the town.

Taprell House's origins are uncertain. One theory is that it was built in the mid-sixteenth century, whilst other suggestions are that it is early seventeenth century. Features in the building relate to both periods, but alterations made, probably in the mid-eighteenth century, make positive identification difficult. Another theory is that Taprell House was built at the beginning of the seventeenth century using dressed stone from the then ruinous Restormel Castle. No definite conclusions have been reached, so it is something of a case of 'make your own choice' when it comes to the origin.

The Taprell family, after whom the house took its name, are thought to have originated in the St Neot area, where they were tinners, and it was probably from this that they became wealthy. The first mention of them is of Ralph Taprell, who is mentioned as being in the Lostwithiel area around 1603 and being of some standing in the town. Their move from a comparatively remote mining area to a quite important town is a sign of the Taprell family 'going up in the world'.

Members of the family soon became prominent in the town: they held between them the office of Mayor of Lostwithiel fifteen or sixteen times and were mentioned many times as burgesses, but were unfortunately sometimes the subject of scandal and shady dealings concerning leases, so power probably went to their heads, making them the 'wide boys' of their time.

The Lostwithiel branch of the Taprells appears to have died out by the middle of the eighteenth century. Taprell House was bought by the first Baron Edgcumbe of Mount Edgcumbe, the estate just across the water from Plymouth, and after being extensively altered and 'modernised' it became known as Edgecumbe House.

By the end of the nineteenth century the front of the building had become a shop; in 1911 the property was sold. The front section of the building continued in use as a shop, but the rear part (Taprell House) fell into extreme disrepair. In 1934 the town council bought the building and after that it had a variety of uses and became even more dilapidated; it was lucky not to have been demolished. However, its historic value was appreciated in time and major restoration work began in 1991 and now the venerable building houses not only the county library but also an exhibition gallery and the town's Methodist chapel, so it has retrieved something of its former glory. It is now appreciated as a valuable and historically important structure.

Despite its decline over the years, its resuscitation means that Taprell House retains much of its early elegance and is recognised today as an important historic building.

Taprell House, Lostwithiel.

The Duchy Palace – A former real palace

It looks pretty dilapidated today, but the Duchy Palace in Lostwithiel is one of the most important historic buildings in Cornwall and efforts are being made to restore it. It was the administrative centre for the Duchy of Cornwall for hundreds of years. It is big and it is beautiful, even in its present state.

What is now left of the palace is the Masonic Hall, because in the nineteenth century the Fowey Lodge of Freemasons bought it from the Duchy of Cornwall, but with the ever increasing cost of maintaining the crumbling building, they are now seeking to sell it and would like it to be put to community use.

It was once a magnificent building as it is believed to have been built by the Earl of Cornwall in the early thirteenth century as a replica of the Great Hall of Westminster in London. An eighteenth-century print shows a building that was little less than a ruin, but covering a large area of land.

The county assizes were held in the palace until Tudor times. The palace complex covered two acres and consisted of the Great Hall and Convocation Hall for Stannary and other county businesses. By 1338 the earldom had been promoted to a dukedom and after that the building became the administration and only polling centre for the whole of the county of Cornwall.

In 1533 the famous writer John Leland, who chronicled so much of the county, wrote, 'in Lostwithiel is the Shire Hall for Cornwall and the Shire Town for Cornwall.' Sadly, not long after that the town began to go into a long and slow decline and its fate was sealed by the Civil War. In September 1644 the Earl of Essex made Lostwithiel his headquarters and great battles ensued in and around the town. The Great Hall was sacked and burnt and the next catastrophe to hit the town was the silting up of the river, which caused the death of Lostwitiel as a port; it had at one time been one of the South West's busiest ports.

Now there are efforts being made to bring the palace back to life, but historic buildings do not come cheap and the purchase and restoration costs have been estimated at £700,000. Both the Freemasons and Lostwithiel Town Council would like to see it put to a use to benefit the community. Both the Duchy of Cornwall and English Heritage are, at the time of writing, exploring ways of ensuring its future.

The building can be seen in the centre of the town as one walks around, and its dilapidation today is very evident; it needs a lot of imagination to picture its former glory. Nevertheless, it remains one of the most important secular buildings in the county. It certainly deserves being brought back to life and shorn of its later additions.

The Duchy Palace,
Lostwithiel.

Restormel Castle – a lovely setting

Perched on its high hill in solitary majesty, Restormel Castle is the embodiment of a medieval fairytale castle; Arthur Mee called it 'one of the Seven Wonders of Cornwall', and he was not far wrong. With its 100yd round circular battlemented parapet and surrounded by a deep moat 50ft wide, it must have seemed impregnable. Nowadays one can stroll on the beautifully manicured grass within those forbidding walls 8ft thick and over 25ft high – but it was not always so.

The Normans built this distinctive edifice somewhere around the year 1100 and the round walls were constructed in about 1200 prior to the addition of the inner walls about 100 years later, along with the accommodating domestic apartments such as a kitchen, bedchambers, a hall and solar.

While in the hands of the powerful Norman lords it became more or less tied to the expanding tin industry and, in the late twelfth century, it came into the hands of Robert de Cardiman. He got Royal permission to hold weekly markets in Lostwithiel and the seat of power moved from there to Restormel. (*See* **Launceston Castle**)

Restormel Castle, Lostwithiel.

In approximately 1270, Richard, Earl of Cornwall, younger brother of Henry III, brought Restormel and the Borough of Lostwithiel from the last remaining member of the de Cadinan family. He died two years later and was succeeded by his son, Edmund, who set about improving the castle and it is believed that it was in the twentieth century that Restormel took on the appearance it retains to this day.

Edward constructed elegant rooms within the keep and strengthened defences; he even included some almost modern innovations in security, including the old favourite of that period: the trip steps, an example of which still remains in the Launceston town walls to this day.

In 1337 Edward the Black Prince, eldest son of Edward III, became Duke of Cornwall and later took over much of the administration of the Duchy lands. In 1362 Edward made his second and final visit to Restormel Castle, but with his lack of interest in Restormel it gradually became rundown and by the time of the Civil War was in a parlous condition.

It was held by the Parliamentarians in the Civil War until it was besieged by Sir Richard Grenville's Royalist troops and captured. It was never lived in again.

Now, like Launceston Castle, Restormel is administered and maintained by English Heritage and is open to the public. It is beautifully looked after and many of the old features can still be seen. There is a walkway around the top of the keep, affording views of the surrounding countryside. It is a must for all lovers of really ancient buildings.

mithian

Harmony Cottage – Home of Cornwall's most famous portrait painter

For a man who achieved what could almost be described as mercurial heights it was a very humble abode. It may have had roses around the door, but Harmony Cottage at Mithian, in the parish of St Agnes, was pretty basic when one of Cornwall's most famous sons was born there. This simple cottage has had several names over the years – Woodcocks, Blowing House and originally just Opie's Cottage, but modern owners were more romantic and gave it the name by which it is known today: Harmony Cottage.

The now detached cottage was once part of the barton of Trevellas in the ecclesiastical manor of Tywarnhayle. At the time of the birth of John Opie it was actually one of three cottages, which were later converted into one dwelling house. Local legend had it that Opie's father, a mine carpenter, built the property, but research has shown that it is much older.

John Opie was known as the Cornish Wonder. He was born in Mithian, an intensive mining area, in 1761. He had always shown a propensity for drawing and painting and at the age of fifteen he came to the notice of Dr John Wolcot of Truro. The doctor was so convinced that Opie had potential as an artist that he bought the boy out of an apprenticeship as a carpenter and took him to be educated and brought up with the graces of a young gentleman and to be trained as an artist. Dr Wolcot's confidence was not misplaced and he encouraged the boy to paint portraits, for which at that time there was a great demand among well-to-do people.

Dr Wolcot introduced Opie to his friends and wealthy patients, among whom was Mrs Boscawen, an influential personality with contacts at court. That lady provided Opie with one of his earliest commissions and it has been said that between the ages of sixteen and nineteen the young artist produced his best work.

In 1781 Dr Wolcot moved to London, taking John Opie with him, thinking there would be more scope for Opie's work in the capital. It is believed that Opie was not entirely happy in London: he was out of his own environment and it could have inhibited his work to some degree. However, during his first year in London Opie caught the attention of the King, and naturally attracted more clients, but despite this, experts consider that his work gradually went into decline, although he remained as popular as ever as a portrait painter.

In 1783, at a high point in his popularity, John Opie married his first wife, Mary Bunn. Unfortunately it was not a very successful move and the marriage lasted only a short time. Opie suffered another blow when there was financial disagreement with Dr Wolcot, who had expended a small fortune in promoting his protégé and obviously wanted to recoup some of it.

Also, it was alleged that the temptations of London life had had an effect on Wolcot and he lavished money on London prostitutes.

Opie and his wife divorced in 1795, but he continued to paint with unabated enthusiasm. In 1798 Opie married for a second time, this time his spouse was Amelia Anderson, a writer from Norwich.

Fame and prestige followed, and in 1803 Opie was elected Professor of Painting at the Royal Academy. In the winter of 1806/7 he gave four lectures which were met with acclaim, but less that two weeks after the forth lecture tragedy struck and Opie died at the height of his achievements.

To all Cornish people he is still highly revered and admired. From the humble cottage at Mithian he rose to great heights, but probably we shall never know if he really yearned for his little Cornish cottage after all.

Works by Opie are scattered around the world and it would be very difficult to compile a full list of all those that still survive as he was such a prolific painter.

north cornwall

The Mermaids – The twenty-first century personified

In north Cornwall a remarkable underground house has taken shape. The architect is Mr James Trewin of the Trewin Design Partnership of Holsworthy, Devon, and the unique building is situated on one of the most beautiful stretches of coastline in the country.

This underground project was created for a client who wanted something really different, and also an eco-friendly dwelling to complement modern thinking on climate change and the way we should cherish our planet in the future. The mass of the structure is buried beneath natural ground level, but because of the steepness of the land one façade of the building provides dramatic views across the valley. The 15m-high glass façade ensures natural daylight floods in and the sliding glass doors allow access to an elevated deck area overlooking a sunken garden, so in no way will the residents feel claustrophobic or, indeed, any different from living in any other dwelling overlooking the magnificent coastline.

'The Underground House', 2007. (Courtesy of Trewin Design Partnership)

'The Underground House', 2007.
(Courtesy of Trewin Design Partnership)

Penetrating the roof is a stainless steel cockpit that allows unrivalled marine views. Very innovative glazing units in the roof are fitted flush to the lawn above to produce an elegant solution to letting natural daylight into the rear of the building.

Space-age features do not end there. The contemporary interior boasts a marble floor, white walls and a stainless-steel and glass staircase which leads to the cockpit, and to cap it all there is an advanced lighting system with mood control.

It is undoubtedly luxuious, a marvel of modern architecture and design personified. It will probably be a long time before we see every dwelling created in this clever and innovative way, but the underground house is surely one of the most interesting and remarkable buildings in Cornwall.

It is of course privately owned, a family dwelling and not open at all to the public, and as it is a hidden house, those seeking a glimpse of it from afar may not even be able to see it at all!

noRth hill

Trewortha Farm – The earliest buildings in Cornwall

The earliest surviving buildings to be found in Cornwall today are, alas, no more than a low broken circle of stones – or even just the outline of a circle in the grass to identify dwellings where once families of probably twelve to fourteen people lived and thrived. But, thanks to the efforts of two remarkable men, there is still a complete 'Bronze-Age' dwelling in Cornwall, not in a museum, but out on Bodmin Moor in a setting where Bronze-Age people would have once lived and gone about their daily tasks.

The Bronze-Age dwelling built by Graham Lawrence, of Trewortha Farm, and Tony Blackman, a Bodmin Moor historian, was officially opened in 1997. It is the eighth reconstructed roundhouse built in Great Britain and the first on the uplands with stone walls. It is modelled on the nearby roundhouse remains in the same field; it has a diameter of 8m with the walls about 1yd high and 75-100cm thick.

The roundhouse is of invaluable educational interest and is visited by school parties from all over the county. A further authentic touch is added when a fire is lit in the centre of the dwelling using locally gathered tree branches. Its construction is an extraordinary achievement in recreating living conditions of early Bodmin Moor inhabitants, and a great deal of painstaking research went into ensuring that it is as authentic as possible. It is indeed a far cry from the twenty-first-century house.

A reconstructed Bronze-Age dwelling at Trewartha. (Courtesy of Tony Blackman)

padstow

Prideaux Place – A film-maker's dream location

Sedding's *Architecture* states that 'there is scarcely an old manor house in Cornwall more teeming with interest than Prideaux Place'. That says it all and is certainly no exaggeration.

The Prideaux family origins go back to the eleventh century and the present family's younger son, William, is William the Conquerer's great-grandson twenty-six times removed. Their history is far too detailed to be recorded here, but it is quite amazing because the family backed the wrong sides during the English Civil War and the Monmouth Rebellion, but survived (a judicious marriage to Sir William Morice secured the family a Royal Pardon for its activities during the Civil War).

It is, however, the house which attracts everyone – the film makers, the public, even politicians (Baroness Thatcher visited during her holiday in Cornwall when she was Prime Minister). The house has changed very little during the last two centuries. The house as seen today is almost entirely the work of three members of the family: Sir Nicholas Prideaux in the sixteenth century, Edmund Prideaux in the eighteenth century, and the Revd Charles Prideaux-Brune in

Prideaux Place, Padstow.

the early nineteenth century. It therefore combines its traditional Elizabethan architecture with the eighteenth-century Strawberry Hill Gothic inspired by Horace Walpole. The house was originally built by Sir Nicholas Prideaux in 1592 as a typical Elizabethan E-shaped manor and remained so until Edmund Prideaux (inspired by his European grand tour) updated the interior and landscaped the gardens. The interior was further transformed in the early nineteenth-century by Edmund's grandson, Charles, who was a great admirer of Walpole's villa at Strawberry Hill.

The house has eighty-one rooms, of which forty-six are bedrooms, but only six of these are habitable. The house was requisitioned by the US Army during the Second World War, and it suffered shamefully during that period. The rooms at Prideaux Place are, however, quite stunning, packed as they are with antiques and paintings. The former great hall, which is now the dining room, has superb panelling from both the Elizabethan and Georgian periods. A portrait of Sir Nicholas Prideaux hangs over the fireplace. The morning room is in daily use by the family and among paintings on the walls are works by John Opie. (*See* **Mithian, Harmony Cottage**.)

The house holds many secrets. It is reputedly haunted; a ghostly dog enjoys the run of one of the bedrooms and Mrs Prideaux-Brune feels 'quite friendly' with a ghostly boy whom she has seen several times in the old pantry. It also has a secret tunnel. This author had the privilege several years ago of being invited to discover (with the aid of a piece of Bodmin Moor quartz as a pendulum) the line of a tunnel which is believed to stretch from the house to the harbour at Padstow. Some success ensued and the pendulum indicated the passage from beneath the present hall of the house, across the terrace and through the field, leading eventually to the harbour. It is thought that in the troubled Middle Ages the tunnel allowed those who had sought sanctuary at Prideaux Place to quickly get access to the port of Padstow and board ship for a safe haven. Unfortunately, it has not been possible to excavate and explore the tunnel as heavy machinery and very skilled technicians would be needed to excavate it for a long distance and the cost would be prohibitive. But it is there.

Prideaux Place has been much in demand by international film makers. There has been a huge amount of film-making there. A German film company started the trend by using the house and grounds as a setting for a Rosamund Pilcher story, and since then a galaxy of screen stars have performed there. An episode of the television detective series *Wycliffe* was shot there and it has also been the setting for Shakespeare's *Twelfth Night*, in addition to other films shown in many countries.

Prideaux Place is indeed special and something of a one off. Even its herd of fallow deer in the park is thought to be the oldest in the country, and has been dated back to AD 453. Legend has it that if the deer die out so will the Prideaux family.

Prideaux Place is open to the public and most certainly well worth a visit.

penzance

The Egyptian House – A touch of Africa in Cornwall

Penzance is a busy and pleasant Cornish town with some impressive buildings. However, there is one building in particular that causes many gasps of surprise when seen for the first time, because anything less Cornish in a Cornish town could hardly be imagined.

The Egyptian House in the town centre is a real curiosity, the dream of one man. The property is now owned by the Landmark Trust, a charity that restores neglected historic buildings and gives them a new future as holiday accommodation without spoiling their character or appearance. Everybody agrees that they have made a very good job with this property.

The Trust has provided a wealth of history on this remarkable house. The Egyptian House certainly did not start life in its present appearance: it was originally two cottages which were bought for the princely sum of £396 by John Lavin in 1834. He was a Penzance bookseller and obviously a man with an uncanny realisation of the effectiveness of extravagant advertising gimmicks as he had the idea to raise the height of the building and transform its extraordinary pseudo-Egyptian façade. The Trust says that the Royal Arms on the building suggest that it was completed before the accession of Queen Victoria in 1837.

John Lavin bought, sold and exhibited colourful minerals in his shop and also sold maps, guides and stationery. What motivated him to adopt an Egyptian theme is unclear, but it has been suggested that it was possibly intended to emphasise the exotic and colourful side of his geological specimens in addition to being an eye-catcher to attract customers to the shop in an unusual way. (Most of the beautiful and very colourful minerals on sale in the shop in fact came from Cornish mines, but Lavin also imported some foreign specimens.)

In 1822, the entrepreneurial John Lavin married Frances Roberts and they had two sons, Edward and John. His younger son emigrated to Australia where he became a biscuit maker, but died in 1881. Edward ran a stationery, bookbinding and printing business in the Egyptian House alongside his father's mineral shop, renting the premises from his father.

In 1863, a few years after his father's death, Edward sold the entire collection of minerals for £2,500 to the Victorian philanthropist Angela Georgiana, Baroness Burnett-Coutts, abandoned his previous business and, with the proceeds of the sale, built a large hotel on the Esplanade at Penzance.

After the French occupation of Egypt in 1798-9 architects had a greater range of forms available to them and the style appealed to those looking for novelty and publicity – and the Landmark Trust says the Egyptian House would seems to be one such example. It has never been proved who designed it, although Peter Frederick Robinson and Plymouth's John

The Egyptian House, Penzance.

Foulston are the names most often mentioned. However, there appears to be no close link to the Egyptian House with either.

After changing hands several times after the deaths of members of the Lavin family, the building was bought by the Landmark Trust, which acquired it from The National Trust, and at that time it was divided into two flats with two seperate staircases. Little had been done to maintain the building since Lavin's alterations and it was in a very bad state, with the Egyptian façade in danger of collapsing.

Work on restoration and repair began in 1970 and the building was converted into three flats with shops below, giving it a completely new lease of life. It was found that the ornamentation was made of Coade Stone, a popular artificial stone which was manufactured in Lambeth, London and was considerably cheaper and easier to work with than natural stone.

The restoration of the building was a splendid job and it is interesting to stand by and watch strangers' looks of surprise when they see it for the first time. Lavin would be pleased if he could come back today and see how well preserved it is and what a lot of attention it attracts.

Trereife House – Links with Wordsworth and Coleridge

'Architecturally one of the most interesting houses in Cornwall'; those are the opening words in the guide leaflet to Trereife House, home of first the Nicholls and then the Le Grice families since the reign of Elizabeth I. It is an excellent example an early eighteenth-century house; buildings of the period were described as symmetrical and beautiful.

The Nicholls lived at Trereife House as yeoman farmers and then minor gentry since before the early sixteenth century. John Nicholls became a successful Middle Temple barrister in London and is commemorated on a memorial on the wall of Madron Church. He improved the family home quite considerably, as befitted his position, before he died in 1714.

The Nicholls family continued to live at Trereife for several more generations and became prominent citizens in their own area and beyond. In the early nineteenth century Trereife changed hands after the last male member of the Nicholls family died at an early age. His mother, by then a widow, married Charles Valentine Le Grice, by whom she had another son, the first member of the Le Grice family at Trereife. He was named Day Perry Le Grice and it was from him that the Le Grice family now living at Trereife is descended.

Charles Valentine Le Grice, whilst a young man at Cambridge, had been close friends with the poets William Wordsworth and Samuel Taylor Coleridge, and his friendship with Coleridge endured throughout their lives. In his early days Charles Valentine had been

Trereife House.

something of a rebel, enjoying 'wine, women and song', but he eventually became a highly respected clergyman.

Succeeding generations of the Le Grice family have owned Trereife and each one has made some alterations to the house to move with the times and their growing social standing, but at the same time they endeavoured to preserve it as an historical building.

In the interior of the house there are notable examples of sixteenth- and seventeenth-century plasterwork in the ceilings, and the mouldings on the soft wood panelling in several rooms echo this. The original symmetry of the Queen Anne period was at first broken by the Georgian stable wing and the main house. Incidentally, a yew tree outside the dining room is believed to be at least 200 years old.

Trereife is still a friendly family home. It is occasionally open to the public.

Treneere – 'to an old retainer'

An Englishman's home is his castle – even if it is now in close proximity to a modern housing estate – and what better castle could one have than Treneere Manor?

Treneere Manor in Penzance was built in 1748 at the centre of what was then one of the county's finest estates. It is a typical Georgian building with the steps to its north front entrance door not overtly ornate to adorn its exterior. Its interior is, however, a different story, one of its treasured features being some very rare and now listed Edwardian wallpaper – and the building has a rather remarkable history.

Among the eighteenth-century owners was William Oliver, of Bath, the man who introduced the world to the famous Bath Oliver biscuit, and in 1976 the estate was bought by Cornish seafarer Joseph Polglaze. That penultimate private owner had four daughters and when he died he left the house to be shared between them. The last of the daughters died in 1956 and she left the house, all its contents and the extensive grounds to her estate gardener, Reginald Symons.

Mr Symons, a Penzance man, started work as a gardener at Treneere when he was a teenager in the 1920s and he worked in the garden there all his working life. He was particularly proud of the many rare and exotic plants in the garden, which he nurtured with diligent dedication, regarding them almost as 'his children', until he died at the grand old age of ninety-five, tending his plants almost to the last. He was looked upon as a very valued friend and former retainer.

As Mr Symons advanced in age he was unable to do the heavy work he had previously enjoyed and both the house and gardens deteriorated through neglect. A large housing estate was built in front of the house on the former estate land.

Mr Symons died in 2006 and bequeathed the whole of the property to St Dunstans, the famous charity which cares for blinded ex-servicemen and women. It was a magnificent bequest which raised the staggering sum of £1.9 million for the charity when it was sold in 2007.

The house is considered to have one of the most interesting histories of any house in Cornwall and it is hoped it will carry on the tradition and always be a family home.

Treneere Manor,
Penzance.

polperro

Couch's House – Oldest house in the village

One of the oldest, if not the oldest house in Polperro, and described as 'a good example of an early Cornish domestic building', is Couch's house. It is a great attraction to visitors to the popular picturesque fishing village in south east Cornwall. It has hollow walls and a fireplace with an outside chimney.

In the late seventeenth century it was the home of the Quiller family, who owned a fleet of sailing ships carrying cargoes of fish to Genoa and Leghorn in Italy. The Quiller family were also locally famed for playing a distinguished part in the Napoleonic Wars.

Jonathon Couch, surgeon and apothecary, was the village doctor for most of his life and was loved by everyone in the close-knit community. Arthur Mee says he was born and died in Couch's House but other authorities claim that when, in 1825, Jonathon Couch married Jane Quiller, daughter of Captain Richard Quiller (famed as a privateer and smuggle), the couple moved into her parents' former home and lived there for fifty-six years.

Dr Jonathan Couch's house, Polperro.

Jonathon Couch was a dedicated naturalist; he collected fossils and he wrote a famous work entitled *The History of British Fishes*, which was published in 1862 and soon became a definitive work. He also wrote hundreds of articles about the natural world.

Jonathon's famous grandson, the very popular and revered Cornish author Sir Arthur Quiller Couch, used the house as the setting for his novel *Nick Nan, Reservist* and also for his adventure story *Dead Man's Rock*. Sir Arthur lived in Fowey, where his memory is cherished and where he was honoured with the freedom of the town and was its mayor.

Couch's House, with its stone and cob walls, became notorious in connection with smuggling. It is situated by the River Pol, within 100yds of the harbour, and it is reputed that a smugglers' cupboard in the house led to an underground passage, which in turn led to a cave in the outer harbour. It was a perfect smuggler's lair, as the innocent-looking cupboard never attracted the attention of the Revenue men.

The quaint old house has beamed ceilings in many of the rooms and its romantic and exciting history is a great attraction. For many years the house served as a museum crammed with an extraordinary mix of curiosities, including Jonathon's desk – at which he did his writing – and even the shell of a lobster which was claimed to have lived for 300 years!

PORT ISAAC

The Birdcage – home for a thin man!

Port Isaac is a typical old Cornish fishing port and whilst there has been considerable house building in modern times in the neighbourhood, the centre of the crowded little village, with some of the narrowest streets in Cornwall, remains largely untouched.

At one time Port Isaac could boast a quay and breakwater dating from Tudor times, but these have been superseded by a sturdy sea wall, which makes it a fairly safe haven for fishermen.

There were no planning laws in the days when Port Isaac was being created and the little cottages almost tumble on top of each other as though in years gone by every man who spotted a gap of some sort built a home on it.

The most extraordinary of these aged dwellings is known as The Birdcage. It stands aloof and unique on Rose Hill, nestling rather incongruously among the untidy jumble of old cottages in the village's streets. It is remarkably picturesque and cannot be missed. At 200 years old it has withstood the ravages of time and one has to speculate on the inspiration for building it all those years ago. We can only assume that space was so tight that it had to be extended upwards rather than sideways and shaped to fit the space available. The Birdcage is pentagonal and three storeys high. The rooms are tiny – miniscule by today's building standards – and the staircase is just 1ft wide in places, so the original owner would have had to have been fairly skinny.

The accommodation consists of three rooms: a kitchen on the ground floor (which now has a door leading to a small bathroom incorporated in it); a sitting room on the first floor; and a bedroom on the second floor. There is even a small terrace outside, accessed through a door in the present bathroom, so the original owner could presumably have had a pleasant place to lounge in the sun on summer days. The building is believed to originally have been the residence of a cobbler.

The Birdcage is now owned by the National Trust and let as a holiday cottage. There is no space for parking, so it can only be approached by foot, but that would not have bothered the original owner, when a handcart would probably have been the only wheeled transport available. It is a real curiosity, impeccably slate-hung above its whitewashed walls and it is a delight in the bustling little fishing village where it stands out like a sentinel right in the centre. Because of its height, it also stands out prominently when viewed from offshore.

pORt quIN

Doyden Castle – Folly-cum-hideaway

When is a folly not a folly? The answer depends on what interpretation you put on that word. In the eighteenth and early nineteenth centuries every self-respecting landowner had to have a folly on his estate; it was the ultimate status symbol. A folly could have two purposes: it could be a folly pure and simple or its creator may have ideas for it to serve a utilitarian purpose as well. Often follies served as pleasant places to take a seat and admire the view in beautiful surroundings, but in the early nineteenth century Samuel Symons had other ideas.

Port Quin landowner and *bon vivieur* Samuel Symons decided, in 1830, that his folly could serve a very useful purpose attuned to his conception of good living. He therefore selected a dramatic cliff-edge situation in north Cornwall with magnificent views over Landy Day toward The Rumps, and there he built Doyden Castle.

His inspirational folly-cum-hideaway was a little square, castellated building not far from Doyden House, which he named Doyden Castle. The castle was built largely as a place where Mr Symons could entertain his friends to nights of feasting, drinking and gambling – possibly other unmentionable debauchery as well. The castle had a cellar in which there still remains a

Doyden Castle. (Courtesy of The National Trust)

number of large wine bins, which are evidence of times when wine flowed freely and probably contributed to all kinds of 'lively goings on'. As the castle is accessed by a cliff edge track, Mr Symons' guests would probably have been wise to stay at the castle to sleep off the nights festivities before starting to walk home!

Doyden Castle is now owned by the National Trust and has been converted into an unusual and comfortable small holiday home without losing any of its original charm and character. The cellar, or lower ground floor, has (in addition to the wine bins) a kitchen-cum-diner and a small bathroom. The sitting room is on the ground floor and the first floor has one bedroom which provides stunning marine views through its windows.

The castle is a most attractive little building in a totally unexpected setting. Although battered by winter storms, it was built to withstand all that the elements could throw at it and it looks good to stand for a few more centuries to come.

Doyden Castle. (Courtesy of The National Trust)

pRaa sanÒs

Pengersick Castle – the most haunted building in England?

Many houses in Britain claim to be the most haunted property in the country, but Pengersick Castle must come high in the running.

The crenulated tower is all that now remains of the once large Tudor castle. Pengersick was a fortified castle on a site which had a castle on it since the mid-thirteenth century, but the tower, which is now home to Mrs Angela Evans and her son Guy, dates from the sixteenth century.

Mrs Evans and her late husband bought the tower in 1971 after seeing it advertised by the Society for the Protection of Ancient Buildings. At the time the owner was Mr Schofield of Godolphin House, and he readily accepted their offer for the building.

The building and surrounding former garden was in what could politely be described as a seriously run-down condition, and obviously needed a tremendous amount of work to make it habitable. In the 1920s a previous owner had built on an extension tower, a two-storey structure which blends in very well and is not in any way out of place. The previous owner had purchased it from the Duke of Leeds, whose family had owned it and Godolphin Manor for a very long time. In the 1930s it was sold to a single lady who lived there as a recluse and was ultimately found dead there: an event that may have added to the haunting legends.

Mrs Evans and her son now live in the extension and do not find the building at all spooky, although plenty of others find it so.

Arthur Mee tells of some remarkable local legends about the castle. One story is that the castle was built in the reign of Henry VIII by a fugitive from justice. Another is that a rich merchant arrived there, bringing all his wealth on the back of a donkey, and built the castle where the donkey first stopped – as he took that as being an omen that it was the right spot. Although unlikely, it is certainly a romantic story.

The castle's interior was reputed to be lined with wainscoting decorated with paintings. On the wood panelling in the tower is a design of how the castle looked in medieval times. This was fortuitously copied by William Borlase in 1735, a drawing which is now in the Morrab Library in Penzance, and working from it, the present owners are striving to resurrect the enclosed Tudor gardens.

Ghost hunters visit the castle regularly and have recorded some extraordinary sightings. Glowing orbs weaving around one of the bedchambers have been seen by Mrs Evans and some of her visitors, but these manifestations are not said to be alarming. The main bedchamber

Pengersick Castle.

appears to be the most popular room for ghosts and all sorts of apparitions have been seen there by different people.

The site of the original manor house is a few hundred yards from the existing tower and the castle's history is well documented. The earliest reference to it is in 1199, and it is mentioned in the Arundell archives in 1301. The Pengersick family was very well established and wealthy and it is recorded that in 1464 they owned no less than twenty-nine manors in Cornwall and were obviously something of a law unto themselves. One member of the family was executed for plotting the murder of the vicar of Breage and a monk from Hailes Abbey, to which the Pengersick family owed tithe money.

The whole estate now comprises a Tudor house, a medieval castle and an Iron-Age settlement, and Pengerick Castle is open to the public.

st clether

St Clether well and baptistery – A holy place of distinction

This is a very unusual little building, unique in Cornwall. St Clether holy well is tucked away almost out of sight, two miles from the village of St Clether, and is half a mile from the nearest dwelling. It is one of those places that once seen is never forgotten and draws people back time and again.

There are many holy wells in Cornwall and most of them have some sort of little stone structure above them. Some are quite ornate, such as Dupath Well, near Callington, but St Clether has much more – it is the only one with a baptistery attached. It is situated high above the valley of the River Inney 'midst rock crags interspersed with stunted trees and low-growing vegetation, two miles from the northern boundaries of Bodmin Moor.'

It has to be admitted it had not always looked as it does today. In 1894 the Quiller-Couch sisters wrote, 'through neglect this interesting and beautiful well in its wild and picturesque situation is falling into ruin'. These melancholy words struck a chord and stirred into action the imagination of the Devon clergyman Revd Sabine Baring-Gould, and in 1895 he made himself responsible for the restoration of the baptistery (or chapel, as it is sometimes called). He described the state he found it in in *The Cornish Magazine* in 1898, and paints a vivid picture of 'an historic treasure fast disappearing into the realms of total dereliction, soon to be lost from the sight of human eyes'. Revd Baring-Gould was nothing if not a dramatist.

But being able to pen dramatic and inspiring words and being the steadfast and determined man he was, he made up his mind that he was not going to let the inevitable happen. He discovered, in his own words, that, 'the chapel was not the original structure of the apostle and founder, but had been constructed in the fifteenth century'. He immediately set about putting in hand a programme of restoration, on completion of which the baptistery was dedicated in September 1900. The building had an entirely new roof and the upper parts of the walls were rebuilt.

The baptistery stands close to the tiny (supposedly fifteenth-century) well, the waters of which run through the baptistery, flowing under the rough stone altar. The altar is believed to be a good deal earlier than the fifteenth century and on it can be seen consecration crosses, which, although faint, are still visible on close inspection.

Cornish historian Charles Henderson described the well and baptistery as one of the most interesting groups of buildings in Cornwall. Revd A. Lane-Davis, in his book about Cornish holy wells, says the baptistery must have been built by the warden of St Austell because, in 1250, the Avowson of St Clether was given to the chantry of St Michael and St Austell and the well

St Clether holy well.

and baptistery belonged to the Church. At that time they would have been very remote indeed, but they are now within fifteen minutes' drive from Launceston and a pretty half-mile stroll from St Clether churchyard. Nowadays many feet trudge the well-worn path to the well and baptistery, but they still retain their quiet dignity and beauty and are certainly worth the walk to get to them.

st ɗomınıck

Cotehele – A lovely house and gardens

Cotehele is beautiful and steeped in history; it is one of the jewels in the crown of the National Trust properties in Cornwall, a haven of tranquillity and full of interests for all tastes. The house has a warm and friendly atmosphere and is splendidly furnished to reflect its period.

There is so much history attached to Cotehele that it is difficult to know where to start and not so much what to include, as what to leave out. It was always a small independent manorial estate, the medieval owners of which took their name from the place where they had lived since the latter half of the thirteenth century. When William of Cotehele died some time before 1336, his two children, Ralph and Hilaria, became orphans. Hilaria's later marriage to William Edgcumbe sealed the connection with the Edgcumbe family with which the house is ever associated. In 1353 Hilaria brought the property to her new husband, it having come into her ownership when her brother Ralph died childless. The Edgcumbes were a very long-standing Devon family, originally from the parish of Milton Abbot, midway between Tavistock and Launceston, with the River Tamar forming the border between Devon and Cornwall. The house which Hilaria inherited was a quadrangular fortified building and the remains of this survived in the lower courses of the walls surrounding the Hall Court.

After twenty-six years of marriage Hilaria was widowed in 1329, and a year later married William Flete of Sutton, Plymouth. After her death the house was inherited by her son, Peter, in 1411. The Bishop of Exeter granted Peter and his wife Elizabeth a licence to celebrate Divine Worship 'in their mansion in the parish of Calstock'. In 1410 the house was inherited by Hilaria's son, Richard Edgcumbe, and it is his home which is much as we see the house today.

Cotehele has had connections with some remarkable characters, around which have grown local legends which are handed down to the present time. Richard Edgcumbe became Member of Parliament for Tavistock in 1468, but he was a 'loose cannon' and later joined the Duke of Buckingham's revolt against King Richard. He became an outlaw and lived to profit from his rebellion. In Cornish history Richard Edgcumbe has become an almost legendary heroic figure. This man is the subject of a romantic story which is actually probably true.

Richard III's trusted lieutenant, once outlawed, went on the run and lay in hiding at Cotehele. Pursued by the agent of the new King and holed up at Cotehele, the crafty Edgcumbe slipped through the cordon around the house, cut the throat of the sentry and fled towards the river. As the pursuing horsemen almost caught up with the fugitive he took off his cap, put a stone in it and threw it into the river, so his pursuers assumed he had drowned and called off the hunt for him. Richard was actually hiding in the undergrowth and made his way by sea to Brittany.

The gatehouse at St Dominick, Cotehele.

Cotehele House.

A few years later, after the hue and cry had died down, he returned to Cornwall and he built a chapel at Cotehele in honour of St George and St Becket as a thanksgiving gesture – it still stands to this day. It was restored in 1620 and again in 1769 and, after being neglected for a long period, was restored and opened by the National Trust. It is now a charming retreat and pays tribute to the Edgcumbe family up to the present time.

Richard Edgcumbe became a reformed character, prospered and held high office. At one time almost every schoolchild in Cornwall knew the story of Richard Edgcumbe throwing his cap into the river. He lived in tumultuous times when human life was cheap, and he trod the torturous path between villain and hero, emerging at the end as the hero. Richard Edgcumbe died at Morlaix, Brittany in 1489. His tomb had never been located.

Richard's son, Piers, was responsible for the creation of the great hall at Cotehele. He also enclosed the part of Mount Edgcumbe facing Plymouth Sound, and his son, Richard, built a house there in 1553, which became the family seat. It was largely destroyed by fire during the Blitz, but has since been rebuilt and is now open to the public as part of the Mount Edgcumbe Country Park.

There has been so much to write about the Edgcumbes and Cotehele, but it is such an outstanding place and family that it really merits a full history.

st germans

Catchfrench – Inspiration for a landscape gardener

The famous eighteenth-century landscape gardener Humphry Repton worked mainly in the eastern counties of England, but in 1792 he had a commission at Catchfrench, one of a small cluster of jobs he undertook in Cornwall. He was enchanted with it and in his legendary *Red Book* of designs he remarked on the romantic site of the house and the delightful scenery surrounding it. It so inspired him that he enhanced the qualities of the landscape by both opening up Catchfrench to the surrounding landscape and disclosing its inner secrets.

Catchfrench Manor is an imposing Grade II listed mansion in a mixture of different periods, which possibly makes it unique. It was a family seat since the thirteenth century and was rebuilt in 1580, and remodelled in 1716.

The name Catchfrench is rather odd and does not really sound Cornish. There are two explanations for it. One is that it originates from *Cadge Fryns*, which translates as 'the Chief's House'. The other is that it comes from the Norman *Chasse Franche*, which is a rough description of an unenclosed hunting ground consisting of forest or parkland.

Catchfrench Manor.

Few buildings could have had a more chequered history and there are still remnants of its early life to be seen. Part of the Elizabethan house, rebuilt in 1580 by George Kekewich, is now a picturesque ruin, and above the gate to the cobbled courtyard can still be seen the inscription; 'In the year 1580 George Kekewich …' An under-croft of the Elizabethan house is situated under the Elizabethan garden, and it has been converted and dedicated as a chapel.

In modern times the house was divided into flats and after that era was left in a very dilapidated condition. However, in the 1990s it was bought by John and Judy Wilks, who transformed the interior into a beautiful country home with a self-contained staff flat and separate quarters for their elderly parents.

Mr and Mrs Wilks, a deeply religious couple, established the Catchfench Trust working to advance the Christian religion by, as they say, 'spiritual renewal, prayer, teaching, healing and witness'. They opened Catchfrench as a guest house, catering for those with Christian beliefs seeking a restful holiday in idyllic surroundings. They also put into being a ten-year plan to restore the overgrown gardens to Humphry Repton's designs and beauty.

In 2006 the estate was again on the market, Mr and Mrs Wilks having achieved their dream of restoring the house and garden under their ten-year plan. It is hoped that it will be enjoyed as a home for many generations to come; it is a truly historic building.

Port Eliot – Oldest continually inhabited dwelling in the UK

Home to the Earl and Countess of St Germans, the house is one of the most magical and hidden stately homes in England and has a long and fascinating history; it claims to be the oldest continually inhabited dwelling in the UK. It is a Grade I listed building and dates back to the fifth century, although it was substantially altered by Sir John Soane at the turn of the nineteenth century. The Eliot family has lived at Port Eliot since the sixteenth century and Peregrine St Germans is the tenth Earl of St Germans.

The earliest written reference to the estate is in a ninth-century Cornish liturgical fragment in the Bodleian Library at Oxford. The house is so called because it was formerly known as Port Priory and was, in the Middle Ages, a flourishing monastic port. Although it seems impossible today, it is true that for many centuries the house was approached by water across what is now the park. Until the 1890s the old oak tree which stood in the park had a large iron ring in it to which boats were once moored.

The building as seen today is an amalgam of different periods. In places the foundations are ninth century and there are tenth-century windows as well as thirteenth-century English perpendicular windows. In the eighteenth century Sir John Soane masterminded a major 'make over'.

Port Eliot House, St Germans.

The Eliots had become rich at the beginning of the eighteenth century and felt it appropriate to follow the trend and upgrade their property to further enhance it. To make access to the house easier, they diverted the course of the river by building a dam and creating a lake. The Eliots also constructed a new and spectacular drive starting two miles north of the house at Tideford and winding a picturesque route along the estuary. Arriving at such a sumptuous setting, visitors could not fail to be impressed.

In the nineteenth century another intensive makeover took place with two north wings added for the domestic staff and all the necessary domestic offices for a large estate, such as game larders, laundry and sitting rooms for the senior members of the domestic staff. In the nineteenth century, at least twenty servants lived full-time in the house in their own wing of bedrooms, with twice as many daytime staff coming from the surrounding areas.

Since those days little has changed in the fabric of the house, although the domestic arrangements are naturally very different. The main alteration has been that the Round Room has been decorated with a massive mural by the famous Plymouth artist, the late Robert Lenkiewicz. This a most outstanding work of art by a remarkable man, who was eccentric and unconventional to the extreme, controversial and an enigma with a lurid lifestyle, but possessing a talent hardly matched by anyone since the days of the old masters. The mural is something which most definitely should be seen: it is impossible to describe it; one must actually see it and marvel at it.

The first mention of the Eliot family dates from about 1450. In those days the family were landowners in East Devon in the parish of East Coker (now in Somerset), where the famous poet T.S. Eliot is buried.

The Port Eliot family prospered in and around the Plymouth area and in 1563 the priory of St Germans came into the family's hands at the Dissolution of the Monasteries. At that time there was a courtier called Sir Thomas Elyot, who was clerk to the Priory Council and a noted scholar, and it is probable, although not proven, that he may have been involved in obtaining the monastery for his 'country cousins' in far away Devon.

Members of the family have since played a significant role in the development of the country through Parliament. They have always been patrons of the arts and revered for their scholarly activities. The many generations of the family have all left their mark in contributing to the welfare of the nation and more locally.

From March to June 2008 Port Eliot House and grounds were open to the public for the first time. The house contains many notable paintings, including the masterpieces by Sir Joshua Reynolds and Lenkiewicz's wonderful mural. It is a truly memorable place to visit.

saltash

Mary Newman's cottage – the oldest house in town

Mary Newman's cottage is the oldest house in Saltash, but there may be some doubts about the legend which has built up around it.

Mary Newman was the first wife of the famous seafarer Sir Francis Drake, and is reputed to have lived in the cottage as a child. This long tradition seems to have existed since about the year 1820 and there is no reason to disbelieve it – except that there is no proof.

However, the cottage itself is of historic interest and importance. It dates back to about the mid-fifteenth century and is Grade II listed by English Heritage. From the Tamar Protection Societies informative booklet about the property, we learn that there has been a dwelling on the land since the late twelfth century, when the land was held by the Lords of Valletort. They laid out in stitches the area which leads up from the river and encouraged people to settle so as to increase the value of their land holding – today's developers are not a new breed!

The present building is believed to be sixteenth century, although some of the ancient masonry suggests that it could be much earlier. It was last lived in in 1974, when in a very run-down and dilapidated condition, and the Caradon District Council accepted an offer by the Tamar Protection Society to restore it. After years of hard work the refurbished cottage was opened by the Lord Lieutenant of Cornwall in 1984.

Despite its great age the cottage was remarkably intact, having two downstairs rooms and one upper room, accessed by the pole staircase. When it was restored authentic materials were used as much as possible. The cottage is now furnished with period items on permanent loan from the Victoria and Albert Museum in London. Very few simple dwellings from the late Middle Ages have survived in such an intact state.

The garden of Mary Newman's Cottage, overlooking the River Tamar and Brunel's Royal Albert Bridge, is now being restored by members of the Tamar Protection Society and features plants and shrubs, many of them donated, of types and varieties which would have been growing there in the Middle Ages.

Since she has given her name to the building a few words must be included about Mary Newman, who lived from 1552 to 1583. She was born in Saltash, where she lived with her parents, believed to be in the cottage which now bears her name. Living so close to the sea, and to Plymouth, would have been very convenient for her father, described as 'a gentleman mariner' of some repute. Mary Newman met Drake through her father's naval exploits and they were married in 1579 at St Budeaux Church, Plymouth, on the opposite side of the Tamar to Saltash, but Mary still resided in her parents' cottage at Saltash despite being able to afford a

Mary Newman's cottage, Saltash.

much larger dwelling. Lady Mary Drake, as she then was, died of smallpox at Buckland Abbey, Drake's home near Yelverton, Devon in 1583, and was buried in a vault beneath St Budeaux Church.

Mary Newman's Cottage is still owned by Caradon District Council and is leased to the Tamar Protection Society. It is open to the public at specific times from March to October each year.

Trematon Castle – A fortress with a difference

Cornwall is rich in castles and all are unique and have their own characteristics; Trematon Castle is no exception. The name means 'King's home' and derives from the Cornish words *tre* (a home or homestead) and *matern* (king).

The high position in which the castle stands was fortified in the time of Athelston and he died in 939, so the site has long been strategically important. It is 200ft above Forder Creek on the north side of the River Lynher, about a mile from its confluence with the great River Tamar.

The ruined castle which we now see dates from Norman times, being of motte and bailey design, like Launceston Castle. The oldest part of the present castle is the keep; the walls are 10ft wide at the base, so it must have seemed impregnable in its heyday. Holes in the wall which once supported beams and stone supports for roof timber indicate that buildings once existed in the keep. A sally port and impressive gate tower still exist, the great square gate tower having been built by Edward the Black Prince. Enough of the gate tower remains to give quite a vivid picture of the type of chambers within it, including one in which the Black Prince is said to have slept, although it is hardly the sort of bedroom we favour today. At ground level are sinister dungeons which would have housed prisoners.

Count Robert of Mortain, who built Launceston Castle, also built Trematon and he granted it to Reginald de Valletort, whose descendants held it for about 200 years. They finally sold it in 1272 to Richard, Earl of Cornwall, who was the brother of Henry III. When the earl died in 1300 the castle lapsed to the Crown. It was a highly valuable property, being so strategically important that when, in 1337, Edward III made his seven-year-old son Edward the Black Prince the Duke of Cornwall, Trematon became part of the Duchy estates and remains so to this day.

The prince in his later years fulfilled his obligations by paying several visits to Cornwall and spent some time at Trematon. However, even in those barbarous times, loyalties and friendships were recognised, and some time after his visit to Trematon in 1363 the Black Prince gave the castle to Sir Nigel Loring, who had been his companion during the French Wars. It was a generous gift to reward a loyal friendship.

For another 100 years or so Trematon served as a fortress to repel any raiders coming up the Tamar and a fairly formidable fortress it was, even today in its ruined state it exudes a sense of invulnerability. It was considered such a safe haven that Sir Francis Drake used the castle to store treasures from the Indies, rather like the modern local rumours (not substantiated) that the Crown Jewels were stored in Bodmin Jail during the Second World War.

The castle has encountered remarkable happenings. In 1549, during the Prayer Book Rebellion in Cornwall, Cornish rebels led by Humphrey Arundell took Trematon Castle by

Trematon Castle, Saltash.

treachery and they captured the holder, Sir Richard Grenville the Elder. But that was not to be the end of the castle's adventures. During the Civil War in the seventeenth century the castle was held for the King by the Royalists. Later still it served as a prison.

The castle then fell into neglect, but it had another surprise coming. In 1807 the Surveyor General to the Duchy, Benjamin Tucker, leased the castle from the Duchy for a period of ninety years, and he, appreciating the delightful surroundings, built a Regency mansion with a crenulated parapet within the precincts. He removed part of the curtain wall in order to allow a beautiful view of the river from the house and he also laid out the grounds.

After the expiry of the lease the house was occupied by servants of the Crown: General Porter, Sir Claud Russell and Lord Caradon. After the deaths of Lord and Lady Caradon it became privately occupied and is not open to the public. The setting for a home is extraordinary and the grounds are very attractive. It is a tranquil place to live, but one feels it must be surrounded by ghosts, given its tumultuous past.

ISLES OF SCILLY

The Beacon – A long-time survivor

It is a rather extraordinary structure and it claims to be the earliest surviving example of its kind in the British Isles. So what is it? No less than 'The Beacon', as it is popularly known, off the island of St Martin in the Isles of Scilly.

The Beacon was a daymark, a 'poor relation' of the lighthouse. It had no light, so could not, of course, be seen at night, but it still served a very useful, even vital, service to shipping. It is situated on a promontory called St Martin's Head and dates from the year 1683.

In his work *The Islands of Scilly* published in 1766 and reprinted in 1966, Cornish historian William Borlase says, 'the late Mr Ekines, a considerable Merchant of these Islands, built a round tower 20ft high, and a spire on top of it as many feet more, and plaistered [sic] with lime on the outside, that it might be a Daymark to Ships which fall in with this dangerous coast.'

The Beacon was already very old then and in his book *The Fortunate Isles*, published in 1990, R.L. Bowley fills in some very important facts. He tells us that the tower was actually built by Thomas Ekins, the first steward of the Godolphins, that famous Cornish family of Godolphin House and their estate near Helston. Sir Francis Godolphin was governor of the Isles of Scilly during the Civil War and King Charles stayed at Godolphin House in his escape to France via Scilly from the East.

The tower is hollow and has an internal stone staircase. Over the entrance door is a granite stone inscribed T.E. 1637, but the tower was actually built in 1683. It was originally lime washed, but mariners confused it with St Agnes Lighthouse, which was built in 1680, and so after a shipwreck nearby in 1830, its colour was changed, and in 1891 it was painted with the red and white stripes we see today.

During the Napoleonic Wars from 1793 to 1815 the daymark was also part of a signal station and close to it are the ruins of a building which served at the signal station, the use of which was discontinued in 1810.

The Beacon is no longer open as the staircase is said to be in a dangerous condition, but the whole structure remains a conspicuous landmark of great historic interest and it is hoped it will be preserved for all time.

Overleaf: The Beacon, Isles of Scilly.

SCORRIER

Whitehall Farm – Making mining history

The popular conception of a farmhouse is often a somewhat austere building, probably rambling and draughty and with the kitchen being used as a nursery for animals, probably lambs, being warmed in front of the Aga stove and with a general aura of chaos.

But Whitehall Farm does not fit that picture and anyway it was not a farmhouse throughout its existence. It is an elegant Grade II listed Regency dwelling with fine tooled beams in the kitchen and panelled and part-glazed pine doors that would grace any gentleman's residence. All the bedrooms have original fireplaces which were reinstated after being ripped out at one time.

Originally the house belonged to Lord Falmouth's estate and was rented by tenants. The earliest known occupier was Thomas Wilson, who moved to Cornwall in 1775 from Yorkshire to become the manager of the rich Wheal Busy Mine at Scorrier. The manager of a very productive mine was a man of some substance and he needed a home befitting his position; not for him the humble miner's cottage, but something equivalent to a gentleman's residence.

Mr Wilson also acted like a country gentleman. Not long after he moved into Whitehall, one of his guests was James Watt, one of the most famous and important figures of the Industrial Revolution, the man who, in 1768, invented the steam engine in its present form. In 1777 when Mr Watt was on his first visit to Cornwall to oversee the installation of a steam engine at the Chacewater Mine, he stayed at Whitehall at the invitation of Mr Wilson. He was not the last well-known person to say at Whitehall. Over 100 years later it was the home of the parents of famous Cornish opera singer Ben Luxton, who was a frequent visitor there, and it had dropped its farmhouse title and become Whitehall House.

In recent years Whitehall has been run as a four-star bed and breakfast establishment, but it retains its character and elegance and many of its original features.

Whitehall Farm, Scorrier.

stratton

The Tree Inn – Home of the 'Cornish Giant'?

With parts of the present-day Tree Inn dating from the thirteenth century, the building was originally a manor house belonging to the Grenville family, and in 1643 it was Sir Bevil Grenville's headquarters before he led the Royalists to victory against the Earl of Stamford's Parliamentarians at the Battle of Stamford Hill on 16 May 1643 during the Civil War.

The building, however, is ever associated with the Cornish Giant, Anthony Payne, who was an outstanding man in every respect. He was born in 1610 and was reported to be 7ft 4in tall, a corpulent man and a very compassionate one. Arthur Mee describes him as 'the most faithful servant a man ever had.' Popular belief is that Payne died in an upstairs room at the Tree Inn and that the floor had to be cut away to allow his coffin to pass through, as it was too big to go down the stairs.

Anthony Payne accompanied Sir Bevil Grenville onto the battlefield in the Civil War. One rather poignant story about him is that while burying the dead after the Battle of Stamford Hill, he was about to lower the body into the grave when the man stirred, and Payne is said to have taken him back to his own cottage where Payne's wife tended his wounds and the man survived.

An inscription on the wall of the Tree Inn tells of the signal overthrow of the Earl of Stamford by the valour of Sir Bevil Grenville and his Cornish army when Anthony Payne was by his side.

From there the story of Anthony Payne becomes a little involved. Legend has it that he died in the Tree Inn, but one modern-day scholar claims that he died in his own cottage on the Stowe estate and even claims to have discovered, by diligent research, the approximate spot where the cottage stood, but details of that research have never been published, so the claim has not been authenticated, and as the Tree Inn was a manor house belonging to the Grenvilles, the Paynes could well have been living there.

The burial register of St Andrew's Church, Stratton, shows that Anthony Payne and his wife died within a few days of each other in 1691. The actual entry reads 'burials – Sibella, wife of Anthony Payne 9th July 1691. Anthony Payne 13th July 1691'. It is curious that they both died within a week of each other and one theory is that they could have been the victims of plague. Such evidence proves that Payne did not die in battle.

Another legend is that Anthony Payne took Sir Bevil Grenville from the Battle of Stamford Hill to be buried in the Grenville vault in Kilkhampton Church, but Sir Bevil died at the Battle of Lansdown, near Bath.

There is more intriguing history about Anthony Payne, most of it authentic. We know that he was buried at Stratton, but apparently in an unmarked grave, and during work on underpinning

The Tree Inn, Stratton, Bude.

the wall of the south aisle of the church in the nineteenth century a huge lead coffin was discovered. It was found to contain the bones of a remarkably big man, but they crumbled into dust on being exposed to the air and what could be salvaged were re-interred, but no record of that episode was kept – another mystery. Anthony Payne was said to have weighed over 450lb, so the big skeleton could have been him.

What can be authenticated is that when Anthony Payne was serving as halberdier on the guns at the Plymouth Garrison the King was so impressed with him that he was made a Yeoman of the King's Guard and His Majesty even commissioned Sir Geoffrey Kneller, the court artist, to paint a full-length picture of him in the ornate uniform of the time; this picture can now be seen in the Royal Cornwall Museum at Truro. The picture itself had just such a chequered history as its subject. It disappeared after it was completed and many years later was discovered by Cornish historian C.S. Gilbers at Penheale, Egloskerry, near Launceston, a former residence of the Grenville family. It was found rolled up in a piece of carpet and very dirty and Mr Gilbert bought it for £8. After that it passed through the hands of several owners and ended up in a London salesroom, where someone recognised it as the work of Kneller and it was sold for £800. It later appeared among the effects of Admiral Turcker at Trematon Castle when his chattels were sold after his death and it was bought by Sir Robert Harvey, who presented it to the Royal Institution of Cornwall.

Whatever the truth behind the story of Anthony Payne he will always be associated with the Tree Inn, and people often travel from afar to visit the inn and to perhaps see the room where his body was reputedly lowered through the floor. Certainly he would have been very familiar with the building through his association with Sir Bevil Grenville, and who are we to refute the legend?

stoke climsland

Kit Hill Stack – A unique chimney

Kit Hill rises almost 11,000ft above sea level, dominating the east Cornish countryside, a landmark visible for miles; it means a lot to a great many people in many different ways, and crowning it is its famous chimney; without its chimney Kit Hill would lose a lot of its glamour.

The ornate stack is 83ft high. It is far more grandiose in appearance that the average mine chimney and it was specially designed to be impressive because of its prominent position, a condition insisted upon by the Duke of Cornwall. It was built in 1858 for the Kit Hill Great Consol/Kit Hill United mining operations. It served a steam engine that pumped water and also lifted ore from the deep mine workings to the surface. A tunnel-like flue which carried arsenical fumes crossed on the approach to the main mine shafts and below them is a Bronze-Age burial mound.

Kit Hill Stack, Stoke Climsland.

The elaborate brick-built chimney is a complete contrast to the simple typical Cornish mine chimney which served South Kit Hill Mine further down the hill, which opened in 1856.

When the chimney was erected it was thought it would also serve as a waymark for seafarers if whitewashed. Its design is based on that of an ornamental column at the demand of the Duchy of Cornwall, which regarded a plain stack as being totally unsuitable for such a position. It was a curiosity of the day (and still is) and it caused a good deal of local interest with its revolutionary design for a mine chimney, unseen in the building of other Cornish mine chimneys. The stack provided draught for the boiler house and the long curving flue served the calciner (or burning house) – it was not just a pretty face!

In 1985 Prince Charles gave Kit Hill to the people of Cornwall to celebrate the birth of his son, and it is now managed by the Countryside Services, part of Environment and Heritage of Cornwall County Council, and is freely open to be explored by members of the public. The hill itself has abundant archaeological remains, past quarrying and mining activity, and is rich in flora and fauna.

The Old Rectory – A royal hideaway

The Revd Canon Martin Andrews was rector of Stoke Climsland, near Callington, from 1922 until he retired in the 1970s and he lived in the fine old rectory with its nine bedrooms and four reception rooms. It was build 200 years ago on the site of a priory, which was there from before the Norman Conquest, and parts of the present building date back to the Middle Ages; it is Grade II listed, but it has a particularly interesting modern history.

Canon Andrews had close links with the royal family. He was chaplain to King George VI and our present Queen until he retired in 1969 and became a close friend of members of the family. As a result, every King and Queen since King George V visited the rectory over the years.

The Duke of Windsor was a particularly close friend. The two men first met when the duke was Prince of Wales and also Duke of Cornwall, and he visited the Duchy Home Farm at Stoke Climsland with which Canon Andrews was closely involved. They also had a lot in common; Canon Andrews had been awarded the Military Cross when he served as a chaplain in the First World War and the Prince of Wales had served in the Grenadier Guards in the First World War. The canon took great interest in the welfare of ex-servicemen after the war and, following a visit form the prince in the 1930s, the two men discussed the plight of the unemployed in Cornwall and the Duchy Home Farm was set up to provide employment for ex-servicemen.

When he became King Edward VIII, the prince attended parties at the rectory and was joined on occasions by the future Duchess of Windsor when she was still Mrs Wallis Simpson.

The Old Rectory, Stoke Climsland.

In his autobiography written in 1974 the canon says of his visitors, 'I forget how long my visitors stayed, but after they had gone I was convinced that the prince was deeply in love.' Other royal visitors included King George VI and his Queen, later the Queen Mother, and a well-known photograph shows the King and Queen inspecting members of the local Home Guard in front of the rectory in 1940.

In 1956 parquet flooring was laid in the living room especially for the present Queen's first visit and silk was hung on the bathroom walls. Such gross extravagance after the privations of the Second World War amazed the good citizens of Stoke Climsland and Callington, but they did not have much chance to see it all.

The house stands in thirteen acres of delightful gardens and is well hidden behind high walls and hedges. There is a story that a high screen of bamboos was planted to ensure more privacy for royal visitors and when they came and went the villagers of Stoke Climsland, if they knew of the movements, kept discreetly tight lipped.

With the departure of Canon Andrews, the house's glory days were over. In 1978 the Church of England sold the rectory as it was too large for the new incumbent, and it was renamed Pendragon House. It has sadly come down in the world after its illustrious past and its last use was as a residential home.

At the time of writing the house and grounds are on the market again, to be auctioned with a starting price of £500,000, and its future use remains a mystery. Incidentally, Canon Andrews died in 1988 at the age of 102; what wonderful memories that house had for him.

tintagel

The Old Post Office – A 'switchback' roof

At first glance it could almost be a fairytale gingerbread house with its undulating roof and tiny glass lights in the windows, but the Old Post Office is a solid, very ancient and very interesting building which was erected in the first half of the fourteenth century in what was then a remote hamlet in north Cornwall. Today, the National Trust calls it 'a precious survivor of such an early domestic dwelling in the extreme south west of England'; for the National Trust to deem it 'precious' is a guarantee that it is something special.

And that 'switchback roof'? Over the years the roof gradually subsided because of the weight of the original massive stone slates which came from the nearby Cliff Quarry, it therefore took on a distinctive undulating appearance. Now, however, it is strong and weatherproof and the most picturesque building in the popular tourist village of Tintagel.

As Tintagel grew in size over the centuries there developed in 1841 the need for a post office, and three years later it had one – in the building which is now known as the Old Post Office.

The Old Post Office, Tintagel.

By the late nineteenth century Tintagel had become a venue for tourists and with such a growing crowd of visitors to the village there was a need to modernise it, so many of the old buildings were demolished. In 1895 the Old Post Office faced the same threat.

In 1895 the building was empty, becoming derelict, and was regarded as a development site. It was put up for auction and the General Post Office. moved its business elsewhere in the village. However, a group of local artists led by one Catherine Johns felt it deserved preservation and Catherine bough it for £300 and set about raising funds to preserve it. The selling of prints of painting by several well-known artists helped to bring in cash, notably at a special sale at the studio of artist Helen Thorneycroft and the Society for Ancient Buildings organised repairs by the important Arts and Crafts architect Detmar Blow. The building was in a pretty poor state; the result of the appeals enabled some repairs to be done, but it was not until 1992 that major restoration work took place and with the distinctive undulations in the roof being carefully preserved. English Heritage and the Delabole Slate Co. both gave financial assistance.

Now the Old Post Office is open to the public and has been sympathetically furnished in keeping with its age, much of the furniture and other items coming from old farmhouses and cottages in the area, so truly reflecting the original atmosphere of the time when it was possibly a small manor house centuries ago. The Post Room is equipped in the style of a Victorian village post office, as the post office here was started in Victorian times when the room was rented from the then owner of the old manor house – it was known as a 'letter receiving office' and was staffed by a local grocer and draper called William Balkwill.

The garden has now been restored as near as possible to its original appearance and when viewing the outside of the house note the slate chimney pots atop the huge chimney stacks. The chimney pots are a feature of a number of old houses in north Cornwall, being constructed of four Delabole slates riveted together.

The building itself is constructed of local brown slate which has weathered over the centuries to an even grey. The arch over the entrance door is local granite and local greenstone was used for the window surrounds. The walls are very thick and, as already mentioned, the roof was of heavy stone slates.

The Old Post Office is a delightful and authentic building of its period, wonderfully restored and retaining a very evocative atmosphere which entrances visitors, but one needs to be fairly nimble to negotiate the steep, narrow spiral staircase to the north bedroom. How did those early residents manage it after dark when the only illumination was a faintly flickering rushlight?

TREGONY

Golden Manor – Links with a Martyr

Cuthbert Mayne was hung, drawn and quartered in Launceston in 1577. The house where he took refuge because of his faith is still lived in and still bears relics of the tragic martyr.

Cuthbert Mayne's crime was that he was a Catholic at a time when religious persecution was at its height. He was baptised into the Church of England, but subsequently embraced the Catholic faith when the Reformation took place in England. To ensure their safety everyone had to bear allegiance to the 'reformed' church, with the much loved Latin Mass replaced by the Edward VI Prayer in English. Cuthbert Mayne was only a child when the new rule came in, but in Cornwall there was massive opposition to the Latin Mass being outlawed and it spread throughout the south west of England before being brutally suppressed.

When Queen Elizabeth I came to the throne, replacing the fervent Catholic Mary Tudor, and when in 1559 the Act of Uniformity became law, Catholics found themselves having to choose between their faith and their loyalty to the Queen: make the wrong choice and your life could be in danger.

Golden Manor, Tregony. (Photograph by John Lyne)

The former gatehouse at Golden Manor, Tregony, now a private dwelling.

Cuthbert Mayne.

The Tregian family of Golden Manor in the parish of Tregony were devout Catholics and related to the most influential Catholic family in Cornwall: the Arundells. To cut a long and complicated story short, Cuthbert Mayne took the Oath of Loyalty to the Queen and was ordained and took the Chaplaincy of St John's College, Oxford. However, he was not happy and rejected his Anglican background, went to France – where he was ordained – and returned to Cornwall to lead a covert existence as a Catholic, always under threat of arrest or even death.

Mayne went to Golden Manor to live with the Tregian family, ostensibly as a steward engaged in administering Francis Tregian's estate, but undercover his main task was to support and revitalise the Catholic families mainly resident in mid-Cornwall. It was a dangerous task and ultimately proved fatal.

The crunch came when Richard Grenville became Sheriff of Cornwall. He loathed Francis Tregian and the priest then living at Golden Manor, and he set about ridding Cornwall of Catholics. He besieged Golden Manor with 100 armed men and arrested both Cuthbert Mayne and Francis Tregian, and at the autumn assizes in Launceston both men, along with twenty others, were indicted.

Cuthbert Mayne went to the gallows in Launceston's market square, but Tregian was spared the death penalty and instead was made to forfeit all his property and spent twenty-six miserable years in gaol. After Queen Elizabeth I's death he went into exile in Portugal.

Cuthbert Mayne was the first seminary priest to be martyred and was still declared a saint in 1970. His connection with Golden Manor is still commemorated by Cornish Catholics who meet there each year on the anniversary of Cuthbert Mayne's death, and his skull is preserved at Lanherne Convent.

Even to this day a faint sense of foreboding still pervades the building at Golden Manor, particularly in the downstairs room where, we are told, Cuthbert Mayne was arrested. Golden Manor is privately owned and not open to the public, but can be glimpsed from the road.

trewint

John Wesley's Cottage

This building is usually referred to as John Wesley's Cottage and it has a very special place in the history of Methodism, not only in Cornwall, but also elsewhere. It is, however, really Isbell's Cottage, as living in the cottage in the hamlet of Trewint, after their marriage in 1739, were Digory Isbell (1718-1797) and his wife Elizabeth.

The unassuming little cottage in the parish of Altarnun is a place of pilgrimage for Methodists and is visited by hundreds of people from across the globe because it has a very special connection with the great preacher and hymn writer John Wesley, regarded as the founder of Methodism. The very simplicity of the cottage speaks much for the man who was its most famous visitor.

From the 1730s John Wesley, considered instrumental in founding Methodism, a man of very strong and radical views, went on preaching tours throughout Cornwall. At least two of his followers, both preachers, travelling the country to promote the 'new religion', came over Bodmin Moor to Trewint where they sought overnight lodging. They knocked on a cottage

John Wesley's Cottage, Trewint.

door to enquire where they might find this and were welcomed by Elizabeth Isbell. This began a long and fruitful connection with Methodism, as the Isbells were very impressed with what their visitors were preaching.

Digory Isbell was so moved by the preachers, and by what he read in the Bible of the visit of the prophet Elisha to the Shumanite woman, that he was inspired to build two additional rooms onto his cottage, one downstairs and one upstairs, to be used by visiting preachers when in the district. One of the rooms was named the Prophet's Chamber, and John Wesley was the most honoured of the preachers who came there. Altogether he paid six recorded visits to the cottage.

After the deaths of the Isbells, there wasn't a record of many Methodist gatherings at the cottage until 1932 when a Methodist Union celebration was held there and very heavily attended.

Sadly, the cottage deteriorated until, in 1957, it was in such a bad state that the local council considered demolishing it, but it was saved when the Methodist authorities purchased it for £50, later spending £1,000 restoring it. It was re-opened on Wesley Day, 24 May 1950, when Digory Isbell's great-great-great-grandson, Mr A. Thomas Isbell of Manchester, performed the opening ceremony. On Wesley Day each year celebrations are held at the cottage and it attracts large crowds.

The cottage has been furnished as it would have been in John Wesley's day and most especially in the Prophet's Chamber. Today, the cottage is a preaching place where services are regularly held at certain seasons, and is not just a museum. In the upper rooms cabinets contain many items of Wesley memorabilia which have been donated over the years.

The cottage is open to the public in the summer season and a pretty garden has been laid out opposite, a place which many find a haven for meditation and tranquillity; it is a fitting tribute to John Wesley. It is a calm retreat off the very busy A30 road.

TRURO

The Assembly Rooms – Regency High Jinks

It is always worthwhile to look up at the façade of a building, and the Assembly Rooms in Truro are no exception. This elegant building, only the façade of which now remains, started construction in the late eighteenth century at High Cross in the centre of town, right opposite today's cathedral. It was built as a theatre but had a dual purpose as it could be converted into Assembly Rooms for dances when required. The building also contained a card room and a refreshment room.

What catches the eye today are the plaster medallions which embellish the façade. Right at the top, the bas relief depicts a young woman epitomising youth and gaiety, believed to be either Thalia, the Greek muse of comedy and pastoral poetry, or Minerva, Roman goddess of wisdom. The figure holds in one hand what appears to be a mask and something else unidentifiable in the other hand. The plaster has weathered so badly that positive identification is not possible. Shakespeare is fairly easy to identify on one of the other two plaques, and the other depicts famous actor and manager David Garrick, the matinee idol of his day.

The Assembly Rooms opened in approximately 1789-90 and many famous theatrical personalities appeared there, playing to large audiences. During the Regency period from 1810 to 1820 the building was said to be the venue for all manner of nineteenth-century frolics, some of which are perhaps better forgotten! Masked balls were all the rage at the time and these attracted large numbers of people.

In about the 1860s the Public Rooms were built in Truro and the popularity of the Assembly Rooms declined until they were no longer the 'in' place for entertainment. When they finally closed it is said that some people welcomed their demise, considering them inappropriate premises in such close proximity to a place of worship.

The building now houses offices, but the classical façade is still a joy to behold; a reminder of perhaps more flamboyant days in Truro and certainly still an asset to the city centre.

The Assembly Rooms, Truro.

tywardreath

Trenython Manor – An Italian connection

Many famous international figures have stayed in Cornwall over the years, but a magnificent Palladian-style mansion overlooking St Austell Bay has a more unusual history than most Cornish houses.

In the nineteenth century anyone with enough wealth and influence could realise all their dreams with regard to house building, unhindered by planning rules or any of today's regulations, and that applied to Colonel John Peard, a colourful character who was a volunteer in the various campaigns involving the great Italian soldier and patriot Giuseppe Garibaldi. Probably today Colonel Peard would be called a mercenary; he was known as 'Garibaldi's Englishman', and that Englishman had a passion, in addition to soldiering, for Italian Renaissance art and architecture.

After Garibaldi saluted Victor Emmanuel as the first King of Italy in 1860 he retired to his farm at Caprera, but retained his friendship with Colonel Peard, who then lived in a large period house called Penquite, not far from the site of the later Trenython Manor.

Peard was so obsessed with Italy and its history that he persuaded Garibaldi, who visited him at Penquite, to help in the financing, design and construction of a luxury home in Cornwall based on Italianate design and culture; so Trenython came into being. Colonel Peard and General Garibaldi brought in Italian architects to advise and design on incorporating in the house features reminiscent of the Italian Renaissance.

The structure of the house has not altered to any great extent apart from an annexe used as a chapel by Bishop Gott, who owned the property in the late nineteenth century and who also did even more to beautify the general décor of the rooms. The galleried halls of the house epitomise the somewhat flamboyant Italian taste of the earlier days with wrought-iron sconces and other typical features. Floor-to-ceiling panelling was an innovation by Bishop Gott, providing the house with a fascinating mix of special features from differing ages and cultures.

Trenython Manor is now a fine hotel, so it is possible for anyone to see and enjoy its unique features and lovely setting and to witness the atmosphere experienced by a famous man of history who helped to transform the map of Europe as we know it today.

veryan

The Round Houses – Keeping the Devil at Bay

Veryan has been described as the prettiest village in Cornwall; it is situated on the temperate, almost sub-tropical, Roseland Peninsula and it has one unique feature: its round houses.

The first of these curious little dwellings was built in 1806 by the Revd Jeremiah Trist, vicar of the parish, who, it is said, was appalled by the living conditions of the villagers. During the first twenty-five years of his ministry over 400 people died, due largely, it was claimed, to their living conditions. Cottages were damp and some had rooms so low that it was impossible for a man to stand upright in them. So Revd Trist, in a bid to alleviate the unsatisfactory living conditions, called in a Lostwithiel builder called Hugh Lowe and had him build the round houses. They were built of cob and the smallest of the cottages coast £42, an unbelievable figure today, and each had a conical thatched roof surmounted by a cross.

The local story is that the Revd Trist's initiative had an ulterior motive. He was a man who, like most good Cornish people at the time, lived in constant fear of evil spirits and his round houses were, he believed, a cast-iron deterrent to the Devil and any other evil spirits which might be lurking in the vicinity. The round houses had no north door and the windows were too small for the Devil to squeeze through, and they had round walls so that the Devil would have no nooks or crannies in which to hide in case he came prowling around at night and did not see the crosses on the roofs. If the Devil saw the crosses he would immediately withdraw, but on a dark night they may not be visible and 'His Satanic Majesty' may be encouraged to seek entry into the dwellings.

A less romantic legend is that the buildings were based on the design of the round Kaffir kraals, or round huts in south Africa, but that is not quite as 'exciting' as the original legend, so it is not usually referred to locally.

It is reputed that the cottage, were so popular that they were copied by a village in southern Italy, which was also concerned about the intentions of a highly undesirable visitor.

Two more round houses were built in the village much later in the same century, made possible by money left in the will of one Maria Homeyard to provide homes for widows of seamen. They are beside a road leading to Broom Park. Five round cottages were built in the village altogether; two coming into the village from Tregony, two up the hill leading to Carne beach, and one situated behind the school. In olden times it was claimed that the round houses were so situated at the entrance to the village to act as sentinels against the Devil entering the village.

In modern times one round house, known as Left Round House, has been much enlarged and extended and includes a two-bedroom cottage attached to it. It was on the market in 2006 for a figure in excess of £500,000 – a big jump from Revd Trist's £42 home. It is Grade II listed and enjoys quite spacious accommodation, with plenty of room for the Devil to hide if he decides to visit!

Of course the village had grown considerably since the first round houses were built, now sporting modern bungalow estates and other dwellings, but visitors flock there in the summer months to see the rounded houses and learn their remarkable legends.

Incidentally, Veryan's parish church is the only one in England dedicated to St Symphonan.

Above and left: Round houses, Veryan.

WADEBRIDGE

Trevanion Dovecote – A hidden gem

One of the hidden treasures of Wadebridge, very seldom seen by tourists and not even mentioned in the official town guide, is Trevanion dovecote. It is a lovely little building, a bit out of place perhaps in its present situation, but it has been in its original location since the thirteenth century, so can surely lay claim to its site, being such an ancient resident.

The Columbarium or Culverhouse, to give it its more official names, is now owned by the Cornwall Heritage Trust, an organisation which does valuable work in restoring buildings and maintaining historical sites on behalf of English Heritage and other well-known conservation bodies.

Trevanion dovecote, Wadebridge. (Courtesy of Cornwall Heritage Trust)

According to a magazine article by Captain W. Cleeve published many years ago under the heading 'Old Cornwall' the dovecote was probably built in the thirteenth century (this has since been agreed by other experts). It is believed to have been built around 1260 to house wood pigeons which were farmed for their meat and eggs. The building is of slatey stone and has a domed roof which was restored after the Second World War, along with the top section of the building, the rest of it being in good condition.

Captain Cleeve recorded that it has 150 piercings for holes but that only twelve of them are through holes, and he adds that six smaller holes at the top were obviously used for the supports of the upper ends of the potence which carried the revolving ladder within the building. The writer also claimed that there are only about 132 nest holes, about 100 less than the normal practice, but Arthur O. Cooke in his *A Book of Dovecotes*, published in 1920, describes the number of nest holes as 'totally disproportionate to a building of its size.'

The dovecote is a remarkably sturdy little building, no wonder it has stood the test of time so well. The walls are 3ft thick and 18ft high and its doorway measures 6ft by 3ft, although it is thought that it could originally have been smaller.

There is no certainty about who was responsible for erecting it. According to Cornwall Heritage Trust literature it would have had to have the approval of the Bishop of Exeter of the Prior of Bodmin. The right to keep a dovecote was for many centuries restricted to manors and this was specifically conferred by royal grants and private sales of Cornish manors right down to the seventeenth century, although by that time the English laws on the subject had been much relaxed. So the Trevanion dovecote was probably built for the Lord of the Manor of Hustyn, to which Trevanion belonged in 1256. Alternatively, another writer claimed that dovecotes could be erected close to medieval boroughs, so the Trevanion one could have been in that category.

Despite its great age the Trevanion dovecote faced mortal danger in modern time. In 1985 there was risk of it being demolished when an application was put in to develop the land on which it stood. Fortunately, North Cornwall District Council planning officers were asked to take steps to preserve the dovecote as it is a scheduled monument and the planning committee refused to allow the dovecote to be demolished and so the dwellings were built around it. It now stands in its own little corner and Cornwall Heritage Trust has erected protective railings around it and placed a plaque explaining its history.

Definitely an historic building worth seeing and admiring – small is beautiful.

washaway

Ivy Cottage – It entertained royal canines!

This is an unpretentious country cottage with roses around the door and amidst trees, set against the road, and in passing it one would never feel inclined to take a second – or even a first – look. But this cottage has housed royal visitors and it is Grade II listed as a Building of Special Architectural and Historic Interest.

Ivy Cottage was formerly part of the Pencarrow Estate and was a gamekeeper's cottage. In its ground it has four large historic dog kennels, which are believed to have housed working dogs belonging to members of royal shooting parties who visited the estate. Its appearance is deceptive because it is quite spacious inside and has four bedrooms, which at one time probably accommodated gamekeepers from the royal estates, so it has quite a pedigree; you don't have to look vastly imposing to have an important history.

Ivy Cottage, Washaway.

Pencarrow – Inspiration for a composer

Pencarrow is one of only a few stately homes in Cornwall which are still privately owned. The house typifies all that is best in architecture with its classic Palladian frontage, almost forbidding in its perfection, like a beautifully decorated cake which is too good to cut.

The estate near Bodmin has been owned by the Molesworth family and its descendants, the Molesworth-St Aubyns, since the time of Queen Elizabeth I, after being purchased from the Walker family of Exeter by John Molesworth. Prior to that it had belonged to the long-standing families of Stapleton and Sergiaux, although it most probably looked very different in those days from how it does today.

The present house was begun during the lifetime of the fourth Sir John Molesworth, but he did not live to see it completed and it was actually finished after his death by his son, another Sir John Molesworth, the fifth baronet, who succeeded his father in 1766 and died two years later in 1777.

The interior of the house is as handsome as the outside, but of a different era. It was redesigned to the taste of the eighth baronet, Sir William Molesworth, who at the time of his marriage in 1844 sought the services of the fashionable George Wightwick (1802-1872) to carry out alterations more keyed to the period in which they lived. Wightwick, who was the partner in the famous Devon firm of John Foulston of Plymouth, was undoubtedly 'the flavour of the month' at that time.

Wightwick was into recycling even in those early days and he used fine panelling for the entrance hall which he converted into an elegant library. He further established another innovation of the time: a decorative cast-iron stove.

But the house did not stand still and in 1919 Ernest Newton, a distinguished Royal Academician, was engaged by the thirteenth baronet, Sir Hugo Molesworth-St Aubyn, to modernise the interior of the house and adjacent cottages, and the stables were also altered. It is the result of this work that we see today and the house is full of fine antiques.

There is an interesting musical background woven into the history of Pencarrow. Over 120 years ago it was used as a refuge from grief by one of Britain's best-loved musicians, immensely popular to this day.

Sir Arthur Sullivan, a friend of the Prince of Wales and knighted by Queen Victoria, distraught after the death of his mother and in the depths of despair found solace at Pencarrow, and it was here that he managed to get his life back on track. He was invited to visit Pencarrow by the twice-widowed wife of the late Sir William Molesworth (the eighth baronet, a gentleman notorious as a radical MP). Lady Molesworth was a great music lover and had a deep compassion and desire to help anyone in the musical world whom she could befriend. Sullivan was then

Pencarrow, Washaway.

best known as the composer of the famous *Lost Chord*, but he dreamed of composing 'grand' opera. He had been persuaded by his friend, librettist W.S. Gilbert, to compose for the operetta *Iolanthe* and it was at Pencarrow that he finally found the strength and inspiration to do that. *Iolanthe* was acclaimed as 'a work of joyous genius' and is still popular today.

Sullivan was buried, at the command of Queen Victoria, in St Paul's Cathedral, London, but he will always be associated one way or another with his sojourn at Pencarrow.

There is an interesting sidelight to the property in that the name Pencarrow occurs frequently in New Zealand and Miss Sally Harvey, the administrator at Bodmin's Pencarrow, reminds us that the radical Sir William Molesworth, when he was Secretary of State, encouraged the development of the colonies in the 1840s. It was his younger brother, Francis, who took the lead, developing the Port Nicholson area around Wellington, and New Zealand's first lighthouse was situated at Pencarrow Head.

WERRINGTON

Werrington Park – A 'two part' house

Werrington Park house is particularly interesting because it actually comprises two separate houses joined together.

From the Exeter Domesday Book can be gleaned that at the end of the eleventh century the manor of Werrington was governed by the abbots of Tavistock. The abbots were denuded of their holdings at the time of the Norman Conquest, but by the beginning of the twelfth century the monks regained possession of the estate and it became one of their holding until the Dissolution of the Monasteries by King Henry VII, and in 1540 Henry gave it, along with other properties, to Lord Russell, afterwards Earl of Bedford.

Then there came the Civil War with the dramatic changes which took place in England. Earl Russell conveyed the estate, which, of course, included the house, and by 1618 it had passed to Edward, Duke of Bedford, who proceeded to convey the estate to three men – Edward Woodward, Henry Lucas, and Bartholomew Lucas, who in turn sold the estate to Sir Francis Drake, a nephew of the famous sea captain of the same name.

Drake immediately started making changes and after a while decided he needed a new house and built what was described at the time as 'a faire house' on the site of the old manor house of the monks. Portions of Drake's house still remain and are lived in, at the back of the Georgian mansion which is as it now stands and a passage connects the two dwellings. Thus Werrington Park became two houses made into one.

However, the amalgamation did not take place immediately; much was to happen before then. Sir Francis supported the Parliamentarian cause in the Civil War and in 1644 the King rewarded the loyal and victorious Sir Richard Grenville by granting him in sequestration all the estates of the rebel Sir Francis, and Sir Richard took up residence at Werrington Park. Over what would have been the main doorway to Drake's house is a granite stone carved with a reversed letter 'E', which signified that the occupier supported the Royalist cause; this must have been put there by Sir Richard Grenville when he took up residence.

When in 1646 the Royalist army was defeated and the Prince of Wales and his followers fled west, it is recorded that they took with them 'thirty hogshead of cider from Werrington.' With the Parliamentarian victory Drake had his estate returned to him, but in 1649 he sold it to Mr (later Sir) William Morice.

The first Sir William Morice accumulated a vast fortune and bought many properties from people who had suffered during the war. The second Sir William Morice built the present house in front of Drake's house, thus the front of the building is Georgian and the back is of

Werrington Park house, near Launceston.

seventeenth century origin, which makes it two houses in one. In 1974 a fire badly damaged the Elizabethan wing of the house, but it was carefully and painstakingly restored. Special features of the Georgian house include a magnificent moulded plaster ceiling in the saloon, the work of eighteenth-century Flemish craftsmen, who also created mouldings on the staircase where subjects include a very realistic impression of a dead heron.

In 1775 the estate was purchased by Hugh, Duke of Northumberland, and he had bas relief portraits in plaster of himself and his wife below the ceiling at each end of the main corridor in the house.

The estate remained in the hands of the Dukes of Northumberland, who treated it as a sort of holiday residence or *pied a terre* until it was bought in the 1880s by Mr John Charles Williams of Caerhayes Castle, Cornwall. The present owner is Mr Michael Williams, who lives there with his wife and family.

Being privately owned the house is not pen to the public, but the grounds are occasionally opened for charity events.

Cullacott – A treasure nearly lost

When a house is described as the most important medieval house in Cornwall, and when royalty comes to see it, you know it must be something special.

The old house called Cullacott had been lived in by a succession of farm workers over the years, and when the last one left it was in such a poor state that it was used as housing for calves and a store for farm feeds and machinery.

It was only when the owners applied to the district council for permission to turn it into holiday accommodation that its importance was discovered. It was first listed as a Grade I building in the 1980s, but when the application went in in the early 1990s interest in it grew, but the owners had no idea that things would develop as they did and that the house would become the subject of a £400,000 restoration after it came to the notice of English Heritage.

One corner of the building had already collapsed through the ravages of winter weather, but at the time it did not seem to the owners to be anything of great importance.

The first reference to the house is in the Lay Subsidy Rolls of 1339, when it was referred to as Coulecote, and it is mentioned again in 1408 and 1428, so it was of some importance even back then. The first house was a longhouse, built to accommodate humans and animals under one roof. It was built of cob and stone rubble and the greater part of that house still survives; one half was a cobbled byre for cattle and the other half living quarters for the family living in the house.

In 1579 one Walter Blyghe became the tenant and he made some sweeping changes to 'modernise' the house. He had his name and date carved on the granite lintel of the parlour window and he even installed what was considered the height of luxury for those days – a garderobe! He was a man who had illusions of grandeur. Although the house was comparatively small compared to some of the stately homes of the day, Mr Blyghe decided that it must have a hall for important events when there would be a number of guests, so he had one, albeit a bit miniscule by the standards of the day. In those days all the landed gentry had tapestry wall hangings in their halls. Mr Blyghte was hardly able to rise to that, but he was not lacking in ingenuity and he had paintings done on the walls of his hall. A nail was knocked into the wall above and then a cord was painted, to give the impression so something hanging on the wall. In the dim lighting of those days guests could be forgiven for thinking that Mr Blyghe had adorned his walls with tapestries. Remnants of those early artistic efforts are still there, although they were not revealed until skilled conservators got to work on the restoration. Over the years light smudges of colour had shown through, but the owners had thought it was the scribbling with crayons on the lime-washed walls, done by the farm workers' children.

By the 1640s the Blyghes had left Cullacott and were succeeded by the Bewes family, who made further alterations, including providing two more heated chambers. The medieval builders

Cullacott, Werrington.

had craftily installed a trip staircase with varying height treads to deter intruders and it is there to this day, and still as lethal as it was at the time when it was constructed.

After the departure of the Bewes family Cullacott became a small tenanted farm, and in 1184 the front windows of the hall and parlour were converted into doorways. The old house became a farm labourer's cottage and was finally abandoned in the 1960s when it became cattle housing and an agricultural store for Cullacott farm, owned by several generations of the Mann family, who are still there, living in the large Victorian farmhouse little more than a stone's throw away from the old house.

When the restoration was completed the house had a royal visitor in June 1997 when the English Heritage Commissioners, headed by His Royal Highness the Duke of Gloucester and the commission chairman, Sir Jocelyn Stevens, visited Cullacott during a three-day tour of some special English Heritage sites in Cornwall. The Duke was very impressed with the restoration and posed for photographs with the property's owners, Mr and Mrs John Cole. It was a red-letter day for the little parish of Werrington.

This beautifully restored old house is now available for holiday letting during the summer months.

The Countryman – A premises with many 'lives'

The Countryman is a popular public house at Langdon Cross, four miles north of Launceston, but one would never guess that its past was very different and the origins of the building can hardly be believed by those who drink and eat in it today.

It has been a carpenter's shop, a car repair garage, a filling station and a coach depot before its present makeover. Its history started in the late nineteenth century, when Henry Parnell built a house with a carpenter's shop attached to it. The original buildings are shown in an old photograph taken in 1904. The photograph shows a horse and cart standing outside, a cartwheel in the process of being made can be seen at the carpenter's bench and a young man (who could be an apprentice) proudly displays a newly-made wheel.

In 1910 the original workshop was demolished and a new one built a few yards away. This building was far more substantial and had a second storey which later became comfortable living accommodation. This was in an age when the carpenter and blacksmith were indispensable in any country parish, all the farmers having a great need for both skilled craftsmen in their midst. The original house is unchanged in appearance and is lived in today.

By the 1930s the carpenter's shop also had petrol pumps outside it as the horse and cart era was giving way to the time of motorised transport. The carpentry business flourished until the Second World War, but when it closed down along came someone who saw the future was in motor cars, although many country people still went to town on market day in a pony trap or jingle.

The building then became a car repair garage and filling station. The upper floor living accommodation was accessed by a flight of stone steps at the side, and a small room at the side of the building became a very popular general store where local people could get all their grocery needs without having to go into town, and even the paraffin for their lamps or cooking stoves as electricity had not arrived at many properties.

In its next 'life' the building became a coach depot when North Cornwall Cars moved in, running coaches for tours, private hire, school contracts etc., and the little shop was turned into a business office.

But the time came when the proprietors of that business also retired to a quieter life nearer the sea and an application was put in to convert the premises into a public house. Local reaction to this was mixed; one parish council raised very strong objections, whilst the adjoining parish council welcomed the proposed project. A site meeting attended by both factions and a large number of locals was held and impassioned arguments were put forward by both sides. But North Cornwall District Council gave permission for the conversion and the building eventually became a country hostelry.

The carpenter's and wheelwright's shop at Langdon Cross, which later became a garage and coach depot, 1904.

The Countryman Inn & Restaurant, Langdon Cross, Launceston. (Courtesy of John Neale)

Bibliography & References

BOOKS

Acton, Viv A *History of Truro: From Coinage Town to Cathedral City*, Landfall Publications, 1997

Best, R.S., *The Life and Good Works of John Passmore Edwards*, Truran, 1982

Buckeridge, Lt-Col R.G.D. *Dockare House*, privately printed

Herring, Peter C., *The Archaeology of Kit Hill*, Cornwall Archaeology Unit, 1990

Johnson, Bill, *The History of Bodmin Jail*, Bodmin Town Museum, 2006

Lane-Davies, A., *Holy Wells of Cornwall*, Federation of Old Cornwall Societies, 1970

Mee, Arthur, *King's England: Cornwall*, Hodder & Stoughton, 1960

Rendell, Joan, *Werrington Remembered*, Orchard Publications, 2001

Shaw, Revd Thomas, *Billy Bray Country*, privately printed

Tucker, Kenneth and Doris, *Penfold Manor*, privately printed

NEWSPAPERS & MAGAZINES

Western Morning News
Cornwall Family History Society Magazine
Cornish Life Magazine

OTHER

Bude Museum Archives
Cornwall Family History Society

Cornwall Historic Buildings Trust

Cornwall Reference Library, Truro

English Heritage

Launceston Town Archives

Pencarrow guidebook

Prideaux family archives

Private papers of Mr and Mrs J. Cole

Redruth Old Cornwall Society

The National Trust

Tamar Protection Society

Trelowarren guide book.

Unpublished notes by Canon Andrews

Unpublished notes by the late Dr J. Rowe

Unpublished notes by the late Mrs Betty Worden

Werrington Park Estate Archives

Other local titles published by The History Press

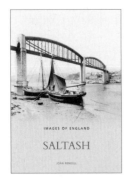

Saltash
JOAN RENDELL

This absorbing collection of old images traces some of the changes and developments that have taken place in the Cornish town of Saltash during the last 150 years. Largely drawn from the Saltash Heritage Centre archive, this volume of over 180 photographs includes rare views of of the construction of the Royal Albert Bridge in 1857 as well as Remembrance Day processions. Aspects of everyday life are also featured, from schools, churches, shops and businesses to sporting events, leisure pursuits and local townspeople.

978 0 7524 3157 4

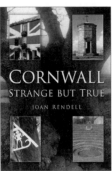

Cornwall Strange but True
JOAN RENDELL

This is a guide to over 100 of the strangest and most remarkable sights in Cornwall. Joan Rendell describes here curious and unusual buildings, objects and landscape features that have survived the centuries. Some will be familiar to residents and tourists; others are almost completely unknown. This book will make fascinating reading for residents and visitors alike, and will inspire many to explore the highways and byways of Cornwall.

978 0 7509 4623 0

Cornwall at War
Memories, Letters & Reflections from the Parish Magazines
ELIZABETH HOTTEN

Covering the Boer, First and Second World Wars, this absorbing book reproduces letters and articles published in parish magazines from across Cornwall between 1889 and 1951. The majority of letters were written by officers to their families, and provide a fascinating insight into conditions on the front line. Likewise, the parish magazine documented changes on the home front, including evacuations, rationing and blackouts.

978 0 7509 5097 8

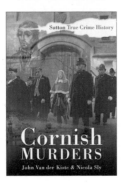

Cornish Murders
JOHN VAN DER KISTE & NICOLA SLY

Cornish Murders brings together numerous murderous tales that shocked not only the county but also made national news. They include the case of Charlotte Dymond, whose throat was cut on Bodmin Moor in 1844; Mary Ann Dunhill, murdered in a Bude hotel in 1931; shopkeeper Albert Bateman, battered to death in Falmouth on Christmas Eve 1942; and William Rowe, brutally killed at his farm near Constantine for the sum of £4 in 1963.

978 0 7509 4707 7

If you are interested in purchasing other books published by The History Press, or in case you have difficulty finding any History Press books in your local bookshop, you can also place orders directly through our website:

www.thehistorypress.co.uk